Magic Lantern Guides

Canon EOS 20D DIGITAL

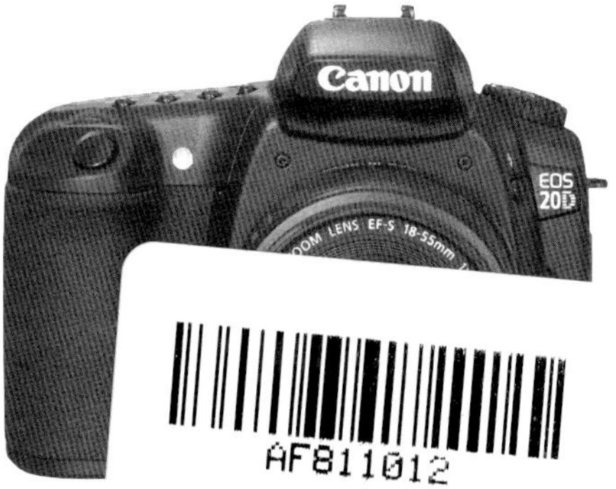

Rob Sheppard

LARK BOOKS
A Division of Sterling Publishing Co., Inc.
New York

Book Design and Layout: Michael Robertson
Cover Design: Barbara Zaretsky
Editorial Assistance: Delores Gosnell

Library of Congress Cataloging-in-Publication Data

Sheppard, Rob.
Canon EOS 20D / Rob Sheppard.
p. cm. -- (Magic lantern guides)
Includes index.
ISBN 1-57990-692-3 (pbk.)
1. Canon camera--Handbooks, manuals, etc. 2. Digital cameras--Handbooks, manuals, etc. I. Title. II. Series.
TR263.C3S522 2005
771.3'3--dc22
2004024499

10 9 8 7 6 5 4

Published by Lark Books, A Division of
Sterling Publishing Co., Inc.
387 Park Avenue South, New York, N.Y. 10016

Distributed in Canada by Sterling Publishing, c/o Canadian Manda Group,
165 Dufferin Street, Toronto, Ontario, Canada M6K 3H6

Distributed in the United Kingdom by GMC Distribution Services,
Castle Place, 166 High Street, Lewes, East Sussex, England BN7 1XU

Distributed in Australia by Capricorn Link (Australia) Pty Ltd., P.O. Box 704, Windsor, NSW 2756 Australia

If you have questions or comments about this book, please contact:
Lark Books, 67 Broadway, Asheville, NC 28801, (828) 253-0467, www.larkbooks.com

Manufactured in China

ISBN 13: 978-1-57990-692-4
ISBN 10: 1-57990-692-3

For information about custom editions, special sales, premium and corporate purchases, please contact Sterling Special Sales Department at 800-805-5489 or specialsales@sterlingpub.com.

Rob Sheppard

Canon EOS 20D

Contents

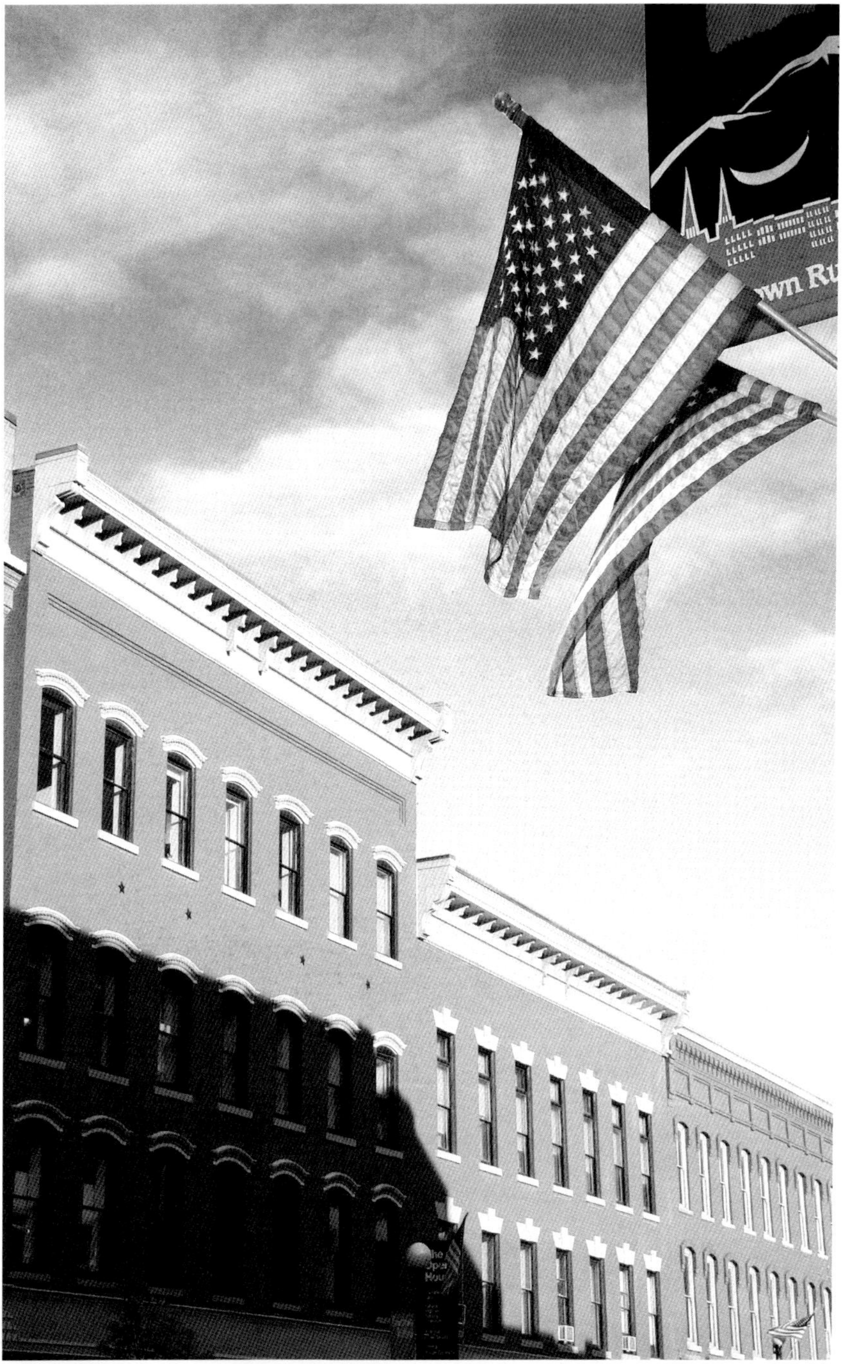

Digital Photography Keeps Getting Better

Quite simply, the Canon EOS 20D sets a new standard for affordable digital SLRs. Introduced at Photokina 2004, this camera is small in size, measuring only 5.7 x 4.2 x 2.8 inches and weighing just 24.2 ounces. Yet the 20D offers 8.2 megapixels of resolution with many additional features that compare favorably with cameras costing much more. While it is the successor to the Canon EOS 10D, it does far more than simply replace an old model. It improves on the 10D in every way, sometimes with dramatic leaps in capability.

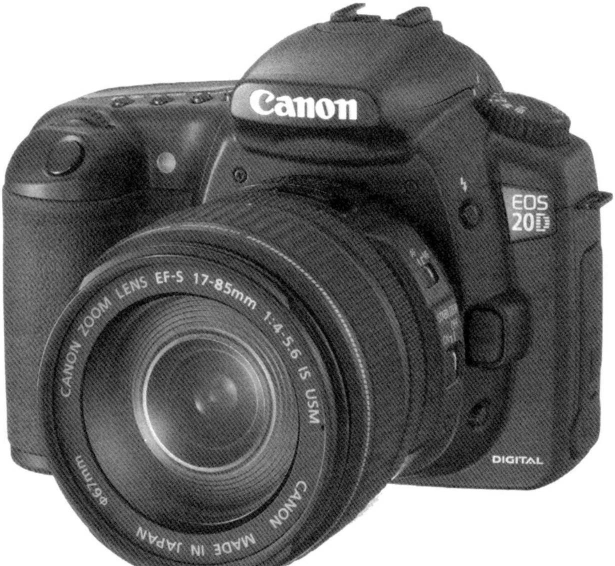

Canon has combined its winning EOS SLR technology with digital photography and delivered a top-performing camera in a medium priced package.

Many photographers have purchased the 20D as an upgrade from an EOS 10D or EOS Digital Rebel. For many others, however, this is his or her first high-quality digital camera. Since, a number of photographers are new to digital SLR photography, we will explain an assortment of topics that are basic to experienced digital photographers (and to any one reading guides to other Canon EOS digital SLRs). If you are familiar with these terms and concepts, skip ahead to the detailed sections on camera operation. As a matter of convenience (and easier reading), we will usually refer to the Canon EOS 20D simply as the 20D.

Canon created this multi-featured camera so that it would meet the requirements of pros and advanced amateurs. You will get the most from the 20D's many capabilities if you understand the key features that distinguish this camera. You don't necessarily need to know how to operate every one of its functions. Once you comprehend a feature, you may decide it is not necessary to master it in order to achieve your desired photographic results. There's no mystical commandment stating that you must become completely familiar with the operational details of every feature. Explore those that work for you and forget the rest. At some point in the future you can always delve further into this book and work to develop your 20D techniques and skills.

Digital cameras do some things differently than traditional film cameras that make them exciting and fun to use, no matter whether you are an amateur or a pro. For digital beginners, many of these differences may seem complicated or confusing. Though most of the features found on a traditional Canon EOS camera are also available on the 20D, there are many new controls and operations unique to digital. A number have been added to increase the camera's versatility for different shooting styles and requirements. The goal of this manual is to help you understand how the camera operates so that you can choose the techniques that work best for you and your style of photography.

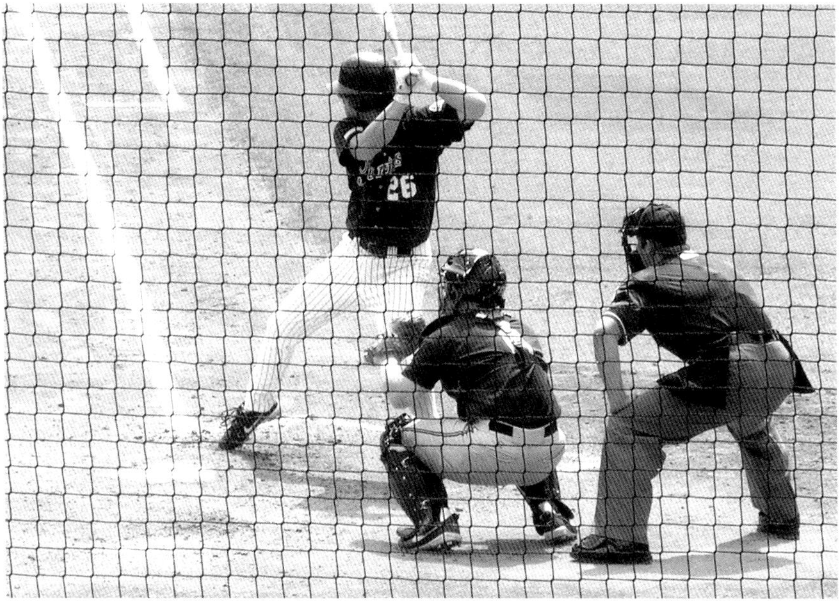

Shooting with a sophisticated digital SLR is a new and exciting experience for many photographers. ©K. Kopp

Differences between Digital and Film Photography

Just a few years ago it was easy to tell the difference between photos taken with a digital camera and those shot with a traditional film camera; pictures from digital cameras didn't measure up in quality. However, this is no longer true. With the 20D, you can make prints of at least 16 x 20-inches that will match an enlargement from 35mm film.

While there are differences between film and digital image capture, there are many similarities as well. A camera is basically a box that holds the lens that focuses the image. In traditional photography, the image is recorded on film and later developed with chemicals. In digital photography, however, the camera converts the light to an electronic image and can do more to the captured image in terms of internal processing.

Film vs. the Sensor

Both film and digital cameras expose pictures using virtually identical methods. The light metering systems are based on the same technologies. The sensitivity standards for both film and sensors are similar, and the shutter and aperture mechanisms are the same. These similarities exist because both film and digital cameras share the same function: to deliver the amount of light required by the sensitized medium (film or sensor) to create a picture you will like.

However, digital sensors react differently to light than film does. From dark areas (such as navy blue blazers, asphalt, and shadows) to midtones (blue sky and grass) to bright areas (such as white houses and sandy beaches), a digital sensor responds to the full range of light equally, or linearly. Film, however, responds linearly only to midtones (those blue skies and green fairways). Therefore, film blends tones very well in highlight areas, whereas digital sensors often cut out at the brightest tones. Digital typically responds to highlights like slide film and to shadows like print film.

The LCD Monitor

One of the major limitations of film is that you really don't know if your picture is a success until the film is developed. You have to wait to find out if the exposure was correct or if something happened to spoil the results (such as the blurring of a moving subject or stray reflections from flash). Sure, you could shoot a Polaroid, but this requires added gear and additional packages of film. The shot you get with the Polaroid image is not the same as the final shot on film.

With digital SLR cameras you can review your image on an LCD monitor, a screen usually found on the back of the camera, within seconds of taking the shot. While LCDs will not reveal all the minute details, they provide a general idea of what has been recorded, so you can evaluate your pictures as soon as you have shot them.

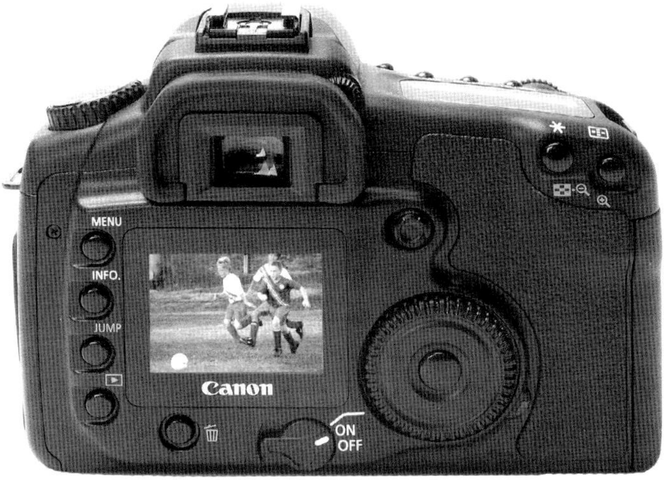

The LCD Monitor is one of the most valuable aspects of digital photography, allowing you to review images instantly after shooting.

Film vs. Memory Cards

Memory cards are necessary to store images captured by a digital camera. These removable cards affect photographic technique by offering several advantages over film, including:

- ***More photos*** — Standard 35mm film comes in two sizes: 24 and 36 exposures. Memory cards come in a range of capacities, and all but the smallest are capable of holding more exposures than film (depending on the selected file type).

- ***Removable photos*** — Once you make an exposure with film, you have to develop and store the negative and print. Due to a chemical reaction, the emulsion layer is permanently changed and thus, the film cannot be reused. With a memory card, you can erase photos at any time, removing the ones you don't want while opening space for additional photos, simplifying the process of dealing with and organizing your final set of images. Once images are transferred to your computer (or other storage medium—burning a CD is recommended), the card can be reused.

- ***Durability*** — Memory cards are much more durable than film. They can be removed from the camera at any time (as long as the camera is turned off) without the risk of ruined pictures. They can even be taken through the carry-on inspection machines at the airport without suffering damage.

- ***No ISO limitations*** — Digital cameras can be set to record at different light sensitivities or ISO speeds. This can be done at any time, and the card in the camera is able to capture images using many different ISO settings. You can even change the ISO from picture to picture.

- ***Small size*** — In the space taken up by just a couple of rolls of film, you can store or carry multiple memory cards that will hold hundreds of images.

- ***Greater image permanence*** — The latent image on exposed but undeveloped film is susceptible to degradation due to atmospheric conditions such as heat and humidity. With new security precautions for all possessions at airports, the potential for film damage has increased. Traveling photographers find that digital photography allows them much more peace of mind. Not only are memory cards more durable, but their images can also be easily downloaded to storage devices or laptops at any time.

The Histogram

One thing that remains true, whether you are shooting film or digital, is that the wrong exposure will cause problems. Digital cameras do not offer any magic that lets you beat the laws of physics: Too little light makes dark images; too much makes overly bright images. Remember, LCD monitors give an essentially instantaneous look at your exposure and, while this tiny version of your image isn't perfect, it will give you a good idea of whether you are exposing properly or not.

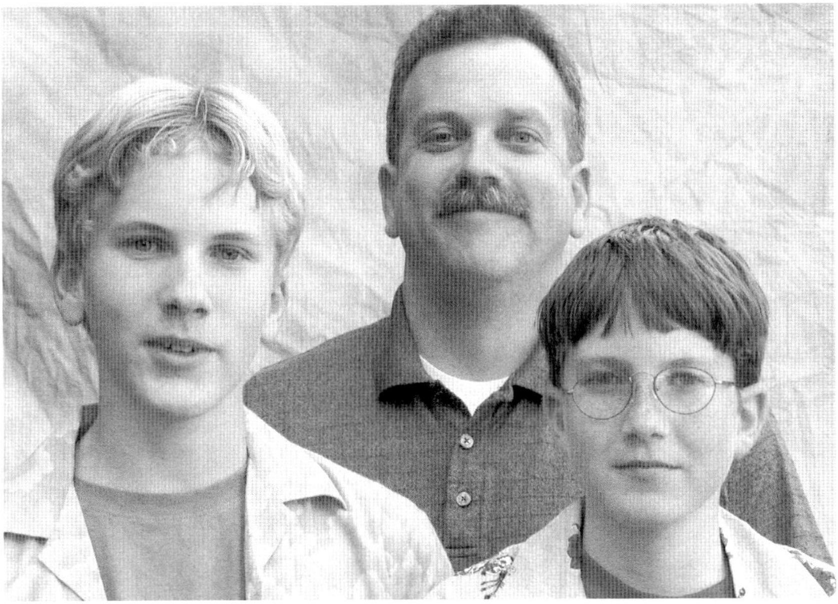

You will always know you "got the shot" when shooting digital because the new technology allows you to determine almost immediately if you have a well composed, properly exposed, and sharply focused picture.

With traditional film, many photographers regularly bracket exposures (shoot the same image several times while changing settings, e.g. increasing or decreasing shutter speed on consecutive shots) in order to ensure they get the exposure they want. You can still bracket with digital if you want, but there is less of a need because you can check your exposure as you shoot. The EOS 20D's histogram function will help in this evaluation. This feature, which is unique to digital photography, displays a graph that allows you to immediately determine the range of brightness levels within the image you have captured.

ISO

ISO is an international standard method for quantifying film's sensitivity to light. Once an ISO number is assigned to a film, you can count on it having a standard sensitivity, or speed, regardless of the manufacturer. Low numbers, such as 50 or 100, represent a relatively low sensitivity, and films with these speeds are called slow films. Films with high numbers, such as 400 or above, are more sensitive and referred to as fast. ISO numbers are mathematically proportional to the sensitivity to light. As you double or halve the ISO number, you double or halve the film's sensitivity to light (i.e. 800 speed film is twice as sensitive to light as 400 speed, and it is half as sensitive to light as 1600 speed).

Technically, digital cameras do not have a true ISO. While the sensor has a specific sensitivity to light, its associated circuits change its relative "sensitivity" by boosting the signal from the chip. For practical purposes, however, a digital camera's ISO equivalent settings correspond to film, so that if you set a digital camera to ISO 400, you can expect a response to light that is similar to an ISO 400 film.

Changing ISO picture-by-picture is easy with a digital camera, but generally not possible with film unless you are willing to constantly reload rolls of varying film speeds into the camera. With a digital camera, you change the "sensitivity" of the sensor using its electronics when you change the ISO setting. It's like changing film at the touch of a button. This capability provides many advantages. For example, you could be indoors using an ISO setting of 800 so you don't need flash, and then follow your subject outside into the blazing sun and change to ISO 100. The 20D camera offers an extremely wide range of ISO settings from 100 to 3200.

Noise and Grain

Noise in digital photography is the equivalent of grain in film photography. It appears as an irregular, sand-like texture that, if large, can be unsightly and, if small, is essentially invisible. (As with grain, this fine-patterned look is sometimes desirable for certain creative effects.) In film, grain occurs due to the chemi-

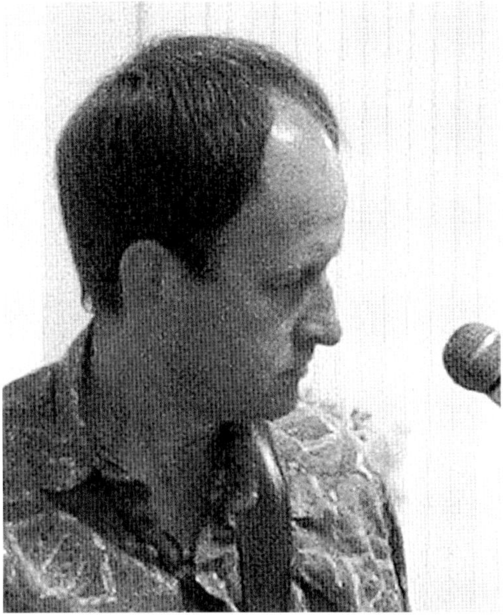

Noise, like that illustrated in this portrait, can occur for a number of reasons in digital images. But the 20D possesses a number of features included to reduce noise.

cal structure of the light sensitive materials. In digital cameras, noise occurs for several reasons: sensor noise (caused by several things, including heat from the electronics and optics), digital artifacts (when digital technology cannot deal with fine tonalities such as sky gradations), and JPEG artifacts (caused by image compression). Of all of these, sensor noise is the most common.

In both film and digital photography, grain or noise will emerge when using high ISO speeds. On any camera, noise will be more obvious with underexposure and may also be increased with long digital exposures in low-light conditions. However, Canon has built advanced noise reduction technology into the 20D. This technology gives the camera incredible image quality at high ISOs with low noise that simply wasn't possible in the past. This camera also has a number of new technologies that create better images with long exposures.

File Formats

A digital camera processes the continuous (or analog) image information from the sensor by converting it to digital data. It converts this data into one of several different digital file formats, including RAW and JPEG.

One very useful feature of digital SLRs is their ability to capture a RAW file. RAW files are image files that include information about how the image was shot but have little processing applied by the camera. They also contain 12-bit color information, which is the maximum amount of data available from the sensor (it is a little confusing that the RAW file format is actually a 16-bit file, though the data from the sensor is 12-bit). The 20D uses the same advanced RAW format developed for the Canon EOS-1D Mark II, the CR2 file, which includes more metadata (data about the image) than before.

JPEG is a standard format for image compression and is the most common file created by digital cameras. Digital cameras use this format because it reduces the size of the file, allowing more pictures to fit on a memory card.

Both RAW and JPEG files can give excellent results. The unprocessed data of a RAW file can be helpful when faced with tough exposure situations, but the small size of the JPEG file is faster and easier to deal with.

Digital Resolution

When we talk about resolution in film, we are simply referring to the detail that the film can see or distinguish. Similarly, when referring to resolution in the context of lenses, we are measuring the lens' ability to separate elements of detail in a subject. Unfortunately, resolution is not as simple a concept when it comes to digital photography.

Resolution in the digital world is expressed in different ways depending on what part of the digital loop you are working in. For example, for digital cameras, resolution indicates the number of individual pixels that are contained on the imaging sensor. This is usually expressed in megapixels. Each pixel captures a portion of the total light falling on the sensor. And it is from these pixels that the image is created. Thus, an 8-megapixel camera has 8-million pixels covering the sensor.

On the other hand, when it comes to ink jet printing, the usual rating of resolution is in dots-per-inch (dpi), which describes how many individual dots of ink exist per inch of paper area, a very different concept. It can be confusing, however it is important to remember that resolution in a digital image is totally different than a printer's resolution.

Dealing with Resolution: The 20D offers three different resolution settings between 2 and 8.2 megapixels. You don't always have to choose the camera's maximum resolution, but generally it is best to use the highest setting available (i.e., get the most detail possible with your camera). You can always reduce resolution in the computer, but you cannot recreate detail if you never captured the data to begin with. Keep in mind that you paid for the megapixels in your camera! The lower the resolution with which you choose to shoot, the less detail your picture will have. This is particularly noticeable when making enlargements. The 20D has the potential of making great prints at 16 x 20 inches and more, but only when the image is shot at 8.2 megapixels.

Digital camera files generally enlarge very well in programs like Photoshop, especially if you recorded them in RAW format first (because there is more data in that format to work with). The higher the original shooting resolution, the larger the print you can make. However, if the photos are specifically for email or webpage use, you do not need to shoot with a high resolution in order for the images to look good on screen.

The Color of Light

Anyone who has shot color film in a variety of lighting conditions can tell horror stories of awful color resulting from the conditions. Color reproduction is affected by how a film is "balanced" or matched to the color of the light. Our eyes adapt to the differences, but film does not.

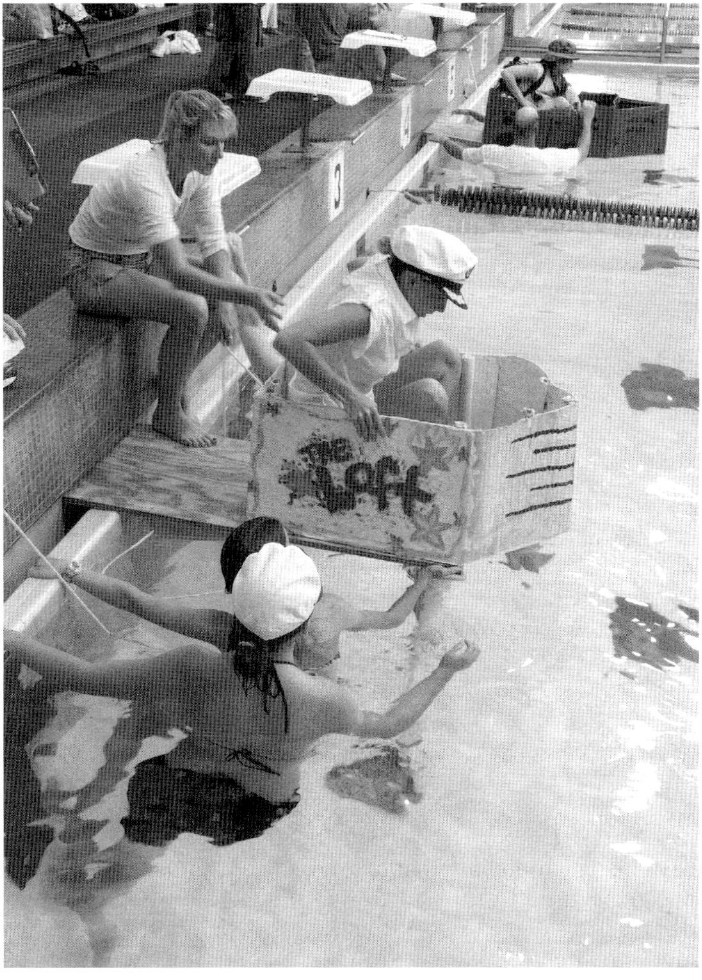

With proper white balance settings, you can get accurate color reproduction even when shooting indoors under tricky or unusual lighting.

In practical terms, if you shoot a daylight-balanced (outdoor) film while indoors under incandescent lights, your image will have an orange cast to it. For accurate color reproduction in this instance, you would need to change the film or use a color correction filter. One of the toughest popular lights to balance is fluorescent. The type and age of the bulbs will affect their color and how that color appears on film, usually requiring careful filtration. Though filters are helpful in altering and correcting the color of light, they also darken the viewfinder, increase the exposure, and make it harder to focus and compose the image.

With a digital camera, all of this has changed. Digital cameras act more like our eyes and create images with fewer color problems. This is because color correction is managed by the white balance function, an internal setting built in to all digital cameras. Long a part of video, white balance has been a standard practice for videographers ever since portable color cameras became available approximately 30 years ago. It allowed the cameras to use electronic circuits to neutralize whites and other neutral colors without using filters.

A digital camera works the same way. It can automatically check the light and calculate the proper setting for the light's color temperature. It can also be set to specific light conditions, or it can be custom-set for any number of possible conditions. Thanks to this technology, filters are rarely a necessity for color correction, making color casts and light-loss a non-issue.

Cost of Shooting

While film cameras have traditionally cost less than digital cameras, an interesting phenomenon is taking place that makes a digital camera a better overall value. Memory cards have become quite affordable. And, once a card is purchased, it can be used again and again. Therefore, cost per image decreases as the use of the card increases. Conversely, the more pictures you take with film, the more rolls you have to buy, the more expensive the photography becomes.

Now with digital cameras there is virtually no cost to shooting a large number of photos. The camera and memory card are already paid for, whether one, ten, or a hundred images are shot. This can be liberating because photographers can now try new ways of shooting, experiment with creative angles never attempted before, and so much more.

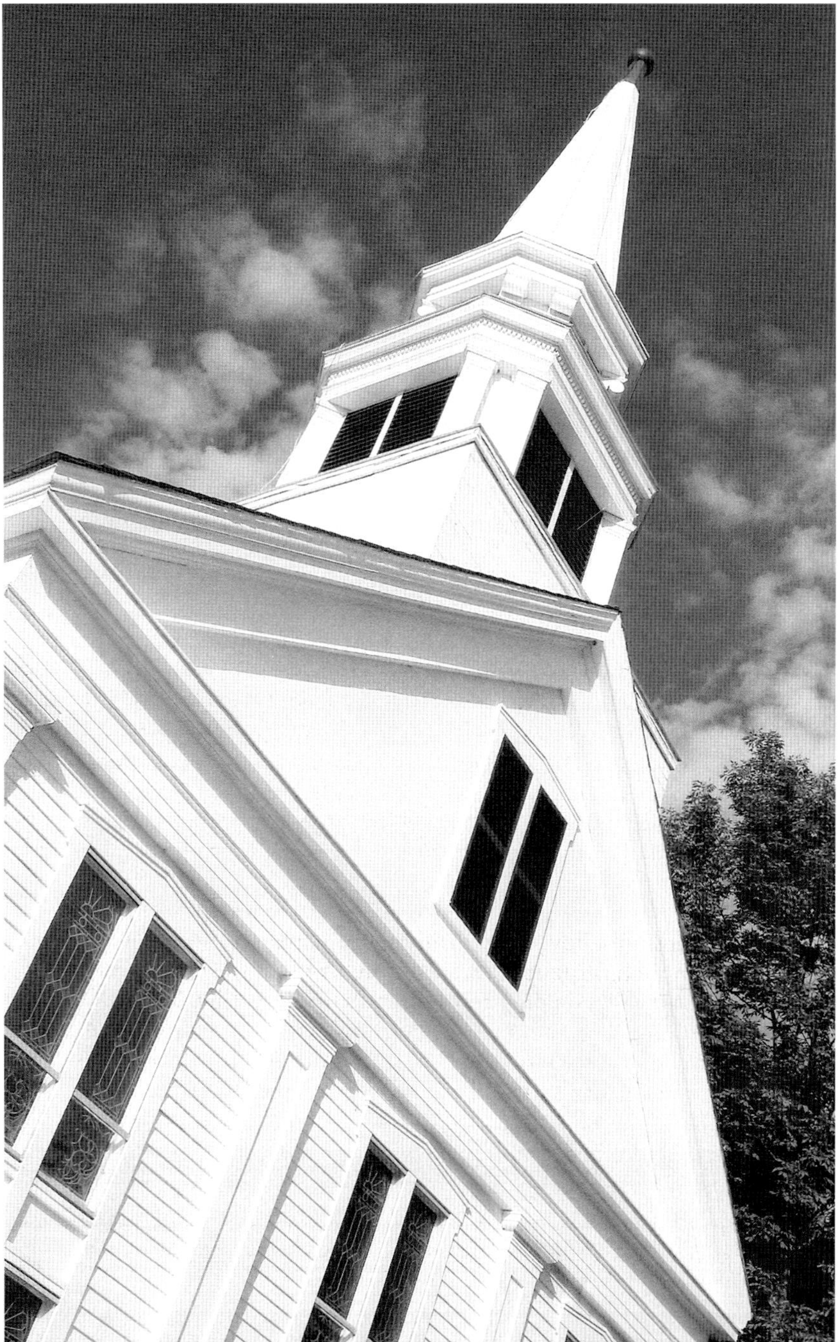

Features and Functions

Camera manufacturers today offer a large number of features with their cameras. They do this to appeal to many buyers, but you may not need or use all of them. This book will give you an idea of what is possible with the many features available, as well as help you best utilize those that are most important. But in any case, you should not feel guilty if you don't use every option packed into this camera! Remember, you can't "waste film" with digital cameras. You shoot as much as you want and then erase those images that don't work. This is important because it means you can literally try out every feature contained on your camera and actually see how it functions. This is a quick and sure way of learning to use your camera, and allows you to choose those that are most useful to you.

The Canon EOS 20D offers a high degree of technological sophistication at a moderate price, in many ways setting the bar for all other digital SLRs in this price range. With a sensor that contains 8.2 megapixels, the 20D shoots 5 frames per second (fps) and up to 23 frames at a time. It also offers quick start-up, fast memory card writing speeds, and other controls that match the performance of recent top pro cameras.

Built with a stainless steel chassis, the camera is housed in a magnesium-alloy body. While more expensive to manufacture, this construction creates a lightweight yet strong unit that is actually smaller and lighter than the earlier EOS 10D. In addition, the shutter unit, mirror box, main mirror, pentaprism, and viewfinder unit are also reduced in size, optimizing them for the small-format sensor (smaller than the frame size of 35mm film). The exterior of the camera is finished with a high-grade, black satin paint with a leather finish.

The versatility of the 20D allows you to shoot totally automatically or have complete control over camera settings so you can be as creative as you want with your photography.

Note: When the terms "left" and "right" are used to describe the locations of camera controls, it is assumed that the camera is being held in shooting position.

Canon has used its EF lens mount for this camera. Introduced with the Digital Rebel (EOS 300D), this mount accepts all standard Canon EF lenses. It addition, the camera accepts compact EF-S lenses, designed specifically for small-format sensors. These lenses can only be used on cameras designed expressly to accept them.

The company engineers reduced the number of parts inside the body, creating an extremely reliable camera. Also, the internal circuitry has been redesigned with fewer components, reducing the complexity and further increasing reliability.

Overview of Features

- Canon-designed 8.2 megapixel CMOS sensor; small-format, APS size
- The technology of the sensor's pixels and micro-lenses enlarges the light sensitive portion of each photosite, improving light-gathering capability and signal-to-noise ratio
- Shoots 5 fps up to 23 frames consecutively at maximum JPEG resolution (6 frames continuous in RAW)
- USB 2.0 interface makes data transfer from camera 11 times faster than EOS 10D
- Start-up time of 0.2 seconds
- Fastest shutter release lag time in its class: 0.65 milliseconds
- High-speed shutter up to 1/8000 sec. with flash sync up to 1/250 sec.
- All-new 9-point autofocus system
- Built-in multi-controller for easy access to AF points
- Improved LCD monitor
- User activated noise subtraction for long exposures
- Fully compatible with entire EOS system of lenses, flash, and other accessories
- FAT32 format permits use of CompactFlash cards larger than 2 GB
- Power-saving design promotes longer battery life

Canon EOS 20D Front View

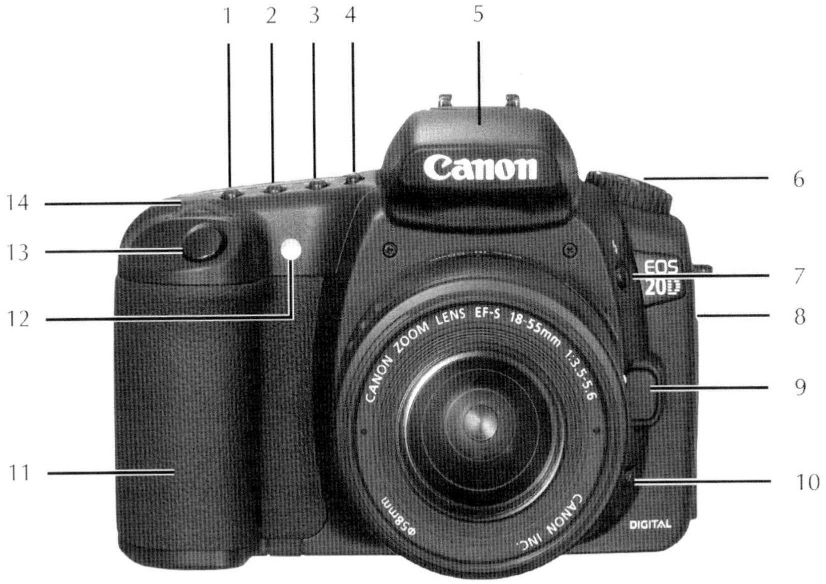

1. *Metering mode selection/Flash exposure compensation button*
2. *DRIVE•ISO (Drive mode selection/ISO speed button*
3. *AF•WB (AF mode selection/White Balance selection button*
4. *LCD Panel Illumination button*
5. *Built-in flash/AF-assist*
6. *Mode Dial*
7. *Flash button*
8. *Terminal cover (side)*
9. *Lens release button*
10. *Depth-of-field Preview button*
11. *Grip (battery compartment)*
12. *Red-eye Reduction/ Self-timer Lamp*
13. *Shutter button*
14. *Main Dial*

Canon EOS 20D Back View

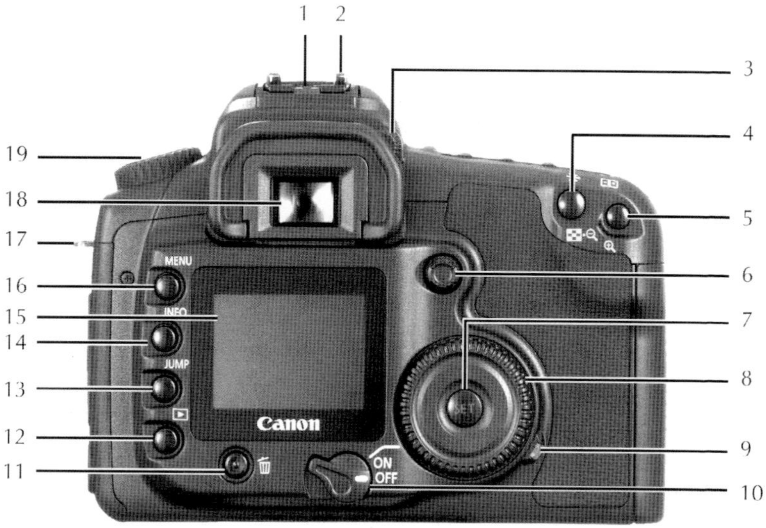

1. *Flash-sync contacts*
2. *Hot Shoe*
3. *Dioptric Adjustment knob*
4. *AE lock/FE lock/ Index/Reduce button*
5. *AF Point selection/ Enlarge button*
6. *Multi-controller*
7. *SET button*
8. *Quick Control Dial*
9. *Access Lamp*
10. *Power switch*
11. *Erase button*
12. *Playback button*
13. *JUMP button*
14. *INFO/Trimming Orientation button*
15. *LCD Monitor*
16. *MENU button*
17. *Strap Mount*
18. *Viewfinder Eyepiece*
19. *Mode Dial*

Canon EOS 20D Top View

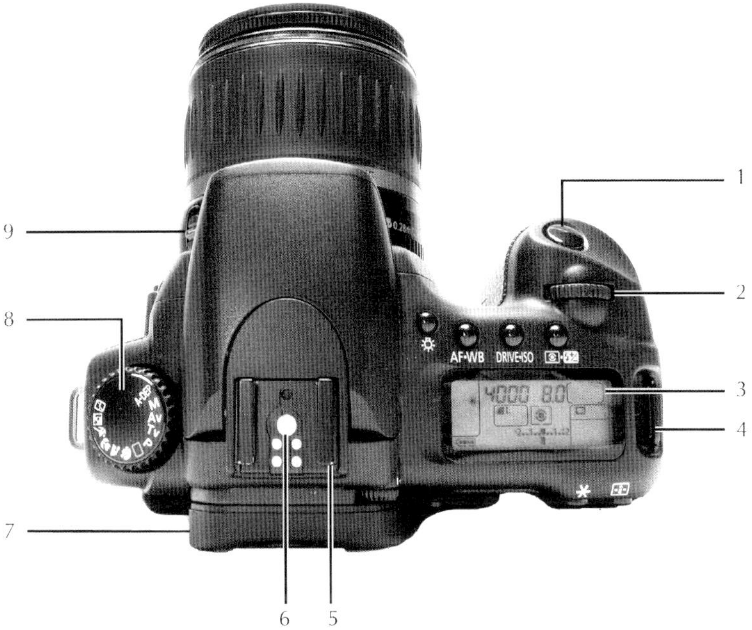

1. *Shutter button*
2. *Main Dial*
3. *LCD Panel*
4. *Strap mount*
5. *Hot Shoe*
6. *Flash-sync contacts*
7. *Eyecup*
8. *Mode Dial*
9. *Focus mode selector (on lens)*

Camera Controls

The EOS 20D uses icons, buttons, and dials common to all Canon cameras. Specific buttons will be explained with the features they control. The 20D often uses two control dials to manage many of the most common and important functions.

Main Dial: Positioned behind the Shutter button on the top right of the camera, this dial allows you to use your "shooting" finger to set things like exposure. The Main Dial works alone when setting shutter speed and aperture. For a number of other adjustments, it works in conjunction with buttons that are either pressed and released or are held down while the Main Dial is turned.

Quick Control Dial: This large, thumb-controlled dial on the back of the camera is used for shooting-related settings and for selecting menu items in the LCD Monitor. It activates for six seconds when an associated operational button is pressed. However, the Power switch to its left controls its functionality. When the switch is in the ON position, the Dial can be used to select the AF point and menu items, or to set white balance, ISO, or flash exposure compensation. With the Power switch set to the angled line (top position), the Quick Control Dial has two additional functions. It can be used to set exposure compensation and to select the aperture in Manual Exposure mode.

Multi-controller: The 20D is the first Canon camera to include this control, which sits just above the Quick Control Dial. It is like a mini-joystick controlled by your thumb. It is used for several adjustments that need multi-directional movement, and is especially useful for AF point selection.

Shutter Button: The 20D features a soft-touch electromagnetic shutter release. Partially depressing the Shutter button activates certain camera functions, such as autoexposure and autofocus. This camera is fast enough, however, that there is minimal speed advantage in pushing the button halfway before exposure. It does help, however, when dealing with moving subjects, to start autofocusing early, so the camera and lens have time to find your subject.

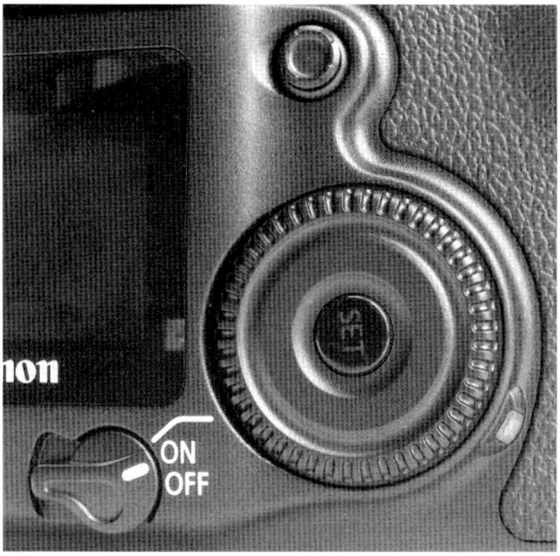

The Power switch, to the left of the Quick Control Dial, turns all camera functions ON or OFF. In its upper position, indicated by the angled line, all functions operate, plus the Quick Control Dial is activated for exposure compensation and aperture selection in M mode.

Camera Activation

Three-Position Power Switch

The 20D has a three-position Power switch found on the back of the camera below the LCD Monitor. The three positions are: OFF, ON, and a special ON that affects the use of the Quick Control Dial. The icon for the third position is simply an angled line. It almost looks like a design element, but it is actually the "On" position for both the camera and the Quick Control Dial for exposure compensation and M mode aperture selection.

Auto Power Off

All digital cameras can turn off after a period of inactivity to conserve power. The 20D has an *Auto power off* selection in the Set-up Menu ꟻT that can be used to shut power after a duration of idleness spanning from one to 30 minutes. If you do not want the camera to turn itself off, set this feature to *Off* and the camera will remain ON as long as the Three-position switch is activated. *Auto power off* is helpful to minimize battery use, but you may find this frustrating if you try to take a picture and find that the camera has shut itself off. For example, you might be shooting a soccer game and the action stays away from you for a couple of minutes. If *Auto power off* is set to *1 min.*, the camera will be off as the players move toward you. Now you try to shoot and nothing happens because the

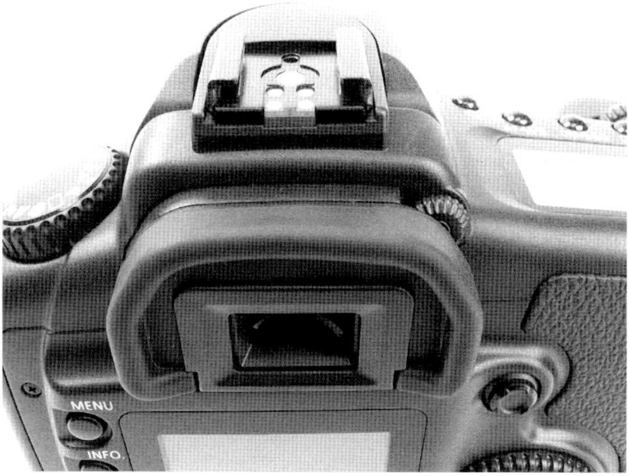

The viewfinder's Diopter Adjustment knob is just above and to the right of the eyecup.

camera is powering back up. You may miss the important shot. In this case, you might want to change the setting to *4 min.* or *8 min.* so that the camera stays on when you need it to.

You access the *Auto power off* function through the menu operation. Press the MENU button (on back of the camera to left of LCD Monitor) and scroll to the Set-up Menu 🔧 using the JUMP button. When Set-up Menu is highlighted (color code yellow), use the Quick Control Dial (the large dial on the back of the camera) to select *Auto power off*, the first option in this Menu. You will be given eight different choices ranging from *1 min.* to *30 min.* (including the *Off* option that prevents the camera from turning off automatically). Use the Quick Control Dial and the SET button (located in the middle of the Quick Control Dial) to choose one of these options.

Resetting Controls

With the many controls built into the 20D, it is possible to set so many combinations that at some point you decide to reset it all. You can restore the camera to its original default settings by going to *Clear settings* in the Set-up Menu.

The Viewfinder

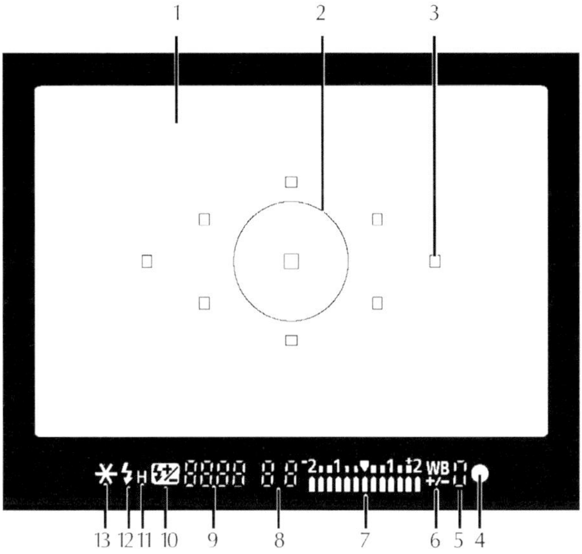

1. *Focusing screen*
2. *Partial Metering circle*
3. *AF point*
4. *Focus confirmation*
5. *Maximum burst*
6. *White Balance Correction*
7. *Exposure level/Red-eye Reduction indicator*
8. *Aperture*
9. *Shutter speed/FE Lock (FEL)/BuSY*
10. *Flash exposure compensation*
11. *High-speed sync*
12. *Flash ready light/Improper FE Lock warning*
13. *AE Lock/FE Lock AEB in progress*

The 20D uses a standard eye-level, reflex viewfinder with a fixed pentaprism. Images from the lens are reflected to the viewfinder by a quick return, semi-transparent half-mirror (there is no cutoff with Canon lenses EF 600mm f/4 or shorter). The mirror lifts for the exposure, then rapidly returns to keep viewing blackout to a very short period. The mirror is also dampened so that mirror bounce and vibration is essentially eliminated. The viewfinder shows approximately 95% of the actual image-area captured by the sensor. The eyepoint is 20 millimeters, which is good for people with glasses.

The focusing screen is a newly developed, non-interchangeable, precision matte focusing screen. This screen uses special micro-lenses to make manual focusing easier and increase viewfinder brightness.

The viewfinder provides 0.9x magnification and includes new superimposition display optics to make information in the viewfinder easy to see in all conditions. The display includes a great deal of data about camera settings and functions, though not all these numbers are available at once. The camera's nine autofocus (AF) points are on the focusing screen, and the solid band at the bottom of the screen shows exposure information, flash information, white balance correction, maximum burst, CF card information, and AF/MF (auto/manual) focus confirmation (a circle appears on the far right when the camera is in focus). Depth of field can be previewed through the viewfinder by using the Depth-of-Field Preview button, near the lens on the lower left front of the camera.

Viewfinder Adjustment

The 20D's viewfinder features a built-in diopter (a supplementary lens that allows for sharper viewing). The diopter will help you get a sharp view of the focusing screen so you can be sure you are getting the correct sharpness as you shoot. For this to work properly, you need to adjust the diopter for your eye. The Adjustment knob is just above the eyecup, slightly right. Fine-tune the diopter setting by looking through the viewfinder at the AF points. Then rotate the Dioptric Adjustment knob until the AF points appear sharp. You should not look at the subject that the camera is focused on, but at the actual points on the viewfinder screen. If you prefer, you can also use the information at the bottom of the screen for this purpose.

Some Canon literature claims you can use this adjustment to see through the camera comfortably with or without eyeglasses, though I have found that the correction isn't really strong enough for most people who wear glasses regularly (like me).

The LCD Monitor

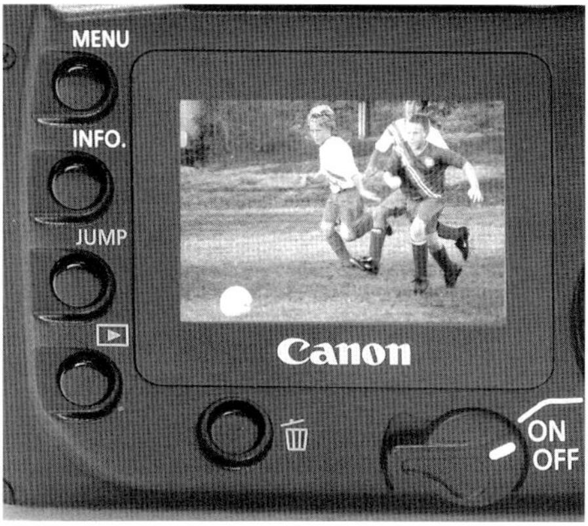

The LCD Monitor in digital cameras is a great tool. You can evaluate and edit your images immediately after shooting. The buttons surrounding the Monitor control numerous functions such as visual display of menus, exposure data, and playback images.

The LCD monitor is probably the one feature of digital cameras that has most changed how we photograph. Recognizing its importance, Canon has put in an excellent 1.8 inch, high-resolution LCD screen in the Monitor found on the back of the camera. With 118,000 pixels, this screen has very good sharpness, which makes it extremely useful for evaluating images.

The LCD Monitor in the 20D can also display graphic representation of exposure values, called a histogram (see page 106). The ability to see the recorded picture combined with an exposure evaluation means that under and overexposures, color challenges, lighting problems, and compositional issues can be dealt with on the spot. Flash photography in particular can be checked, not only for correct exposure, but also for other factors such as the effect of lighting ratios when multiple flash units and/or reflectors are used. No Polaroid film test is needed. Instead, you can see the actual image that has been captured by the sensor.

In addition, the camera will rotate images in the LCD Monitor. Some photographers love this feature, some hate it, but you have the choice. This *Auto rotate* function makes vertical images smaller, but verticals display properly without holding the camera in the vertical position. On the other hand, turning the *Auto rotate* feature off keeps the image as big as possible, but it appears sideways in the LCD.

You can also magnify an image 10x in the monitor in 15 steps (you can set this), and the enlarged photo is scrollable so you can inspect all of it.

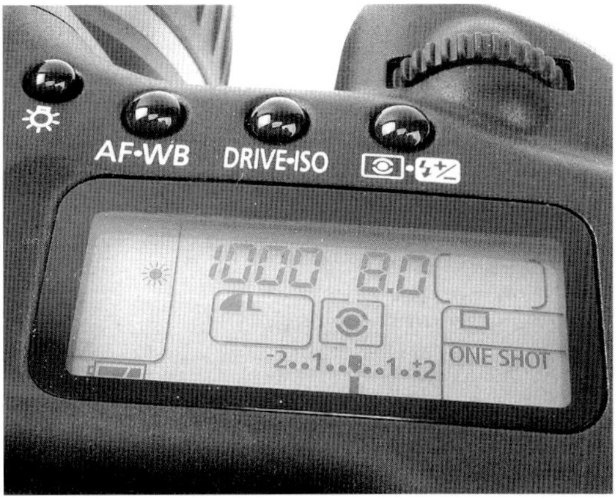

The LCD Panel is on top of the camera. It shows your current shooting information, including shutter speed, image size selection, and AF mode among other camera settings.

The LCD Panel

Not to be confused with the LCD Monitor, the small black and gray panel on the top of the 20D is designed to display shooting information. It sits to the right of the viewfinder and is always operational when the camera is on. It displays information about camera settings, including exposure, white balance, drive settings, metering type, and much more. It can be illuminated in dark conditions by pressing the LCD Panel Illumination button (indicated by a light bulb icon) just above the Panel.

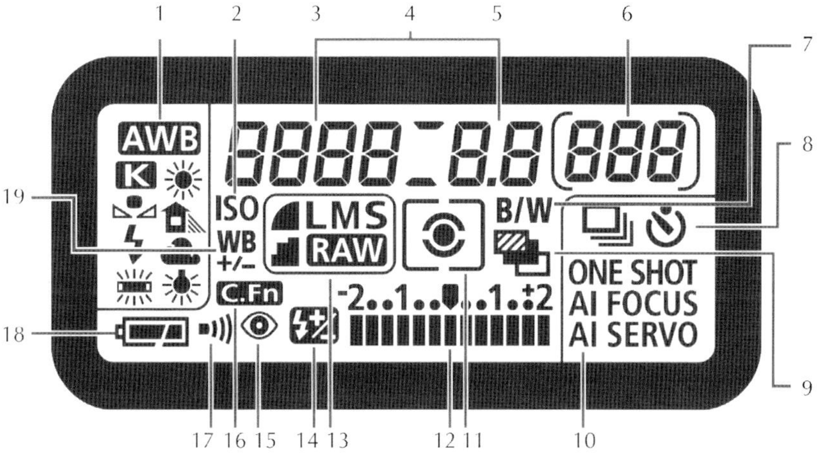

1. *White Balance*
2. *ISO speed*
3. *Shutter speed/buSY*
4. *AF Point selection/CF Card Warnings/Cleaning Sensor/ Processing Parameters*
5. *Aperture*
6. *Shots remaining/Self-timer countdown/Bulb exposure*
7. *Black-and-white/Monochrome shooting*
8. *Drive mode/Self-timer*
9. *Autoexposure Bracketing (AEB)*
10. *AF mode*
11. *Metering Mode*
12. *Exposure level indicators*
13. *Image recording quality*
14. *Flash Exposure Compensation*
15. *Red-eye Reduction*
16. *Custom Function*
17. *Beeper*
18. *Battery check*
19. *White balance correction*

Power

The 20D is powered by a compact Lithium Ion (Li-Ion) rechargeable battery, the 1390 mAh BP-511A (which holds roughly 25% more power than the older BP-511 and BP-512). Milliamp Hours (mAh) indicate a battery's capacity to hold a charge. Higher mAh numbers usually mean longer-lasting batteries.

The camera is designed for efficient use of battery power. However, power consumption is highly dependent on how long different features, such as flash, autofocus, and the LCD Monitor, are used. The more the camera is active, the shorter the battery life, especially with regard to LCD Monitor and built-in flash use. Be sure to have backup batteries (and it is always a good idea to shut the camera off if you are not using it).

Canon estimates that at 68° F (20° C), the battery will last approximately 1,000 frames when flash is not used, or 700 when flash is used 50% of the time. Lower temperatures will reduce the number of shots. In addition, it is never wise to expose your camera or its accessories to heat or direct sunlight (i.e., don't leave the camera sitting in your car on a hot day or a cold one!). Th BP-511A is rated at 8.4 volts and it takes about 100 minutes to fully charge on the CG-580 charger that is included with the camera. It can also be charged in the CB-5L charger used with older cameras, but that charger has a separate cord. The CG-580 is a one-piece compact unit with built-in, foldout power prongs.

Battery Grip BG-E2 attaches to the bottom of the camera and can be used with two BP-511A or equivalent batteries. In addition, the grip has an adapter to allow six AA-size batteries to be used. It also includes a Vertical-grip Shutter button, AE Lock button, and AF-Point Selection button. The AC Adapter Kit (ACK-E2) is useful to those who need the camera to remain consistently powered up (i.e., for scientific lab work). Another power adapter, the CA-PS400, charges two batteries simultaneously, and with the DR-400 DC coupler cord can be used to supply AC power as well.

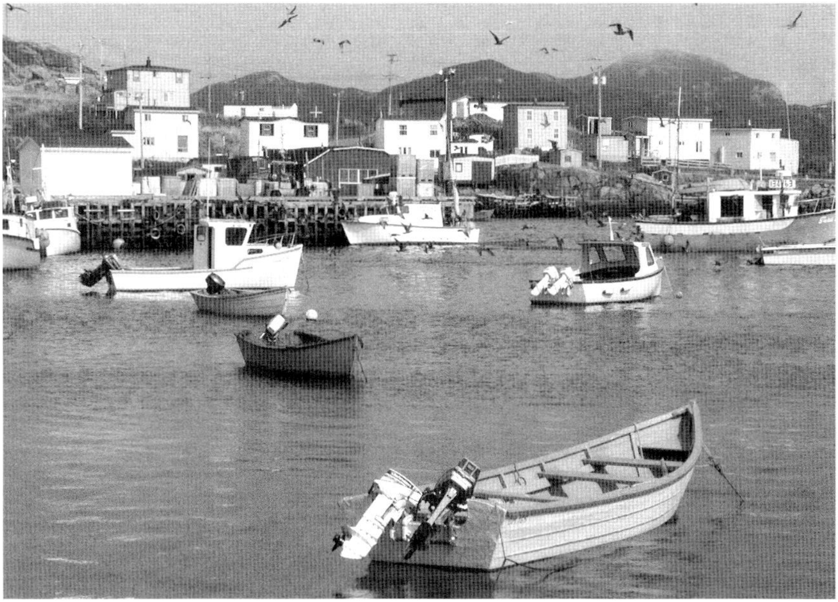

Whether you are looking for shots in your backyard or traveling on vacation, you will want to have extra batteries available so you don't experience "down time" with your camera.

Date/Time

Time and date are established by first going into the Set-up Menu. Next turn the Quick Control Dial to select *Date/Time,* then press the SET button, located at the center of the Quick Control Dial. Continue to use the Quick Control Dial and the SET button to scroll to the current time and date.

A special lithium battery at the left side of the battery compartment holds the date and time "memory." Canon says you shouldn't need to change this very often (the life is about 10 years). It is easy to do—you simply slide the battery holder out and put in a new battery.

The Sensor

The EOS 20D has a newly designed 8.2-megapixel sensor (3504 x 2336 pixels) and it is remarkable in a camera of this class, especially given the 20D's price and speed. It can easily be used for quality magazine reproduction across two pages. I know of *National Geographic* photographers, for example, who use this camera because of image quality and because it is easily portable.

The 20D's Advanced Photo System-sized CMOS sensor, which is the same size as that used for the 10D and Digital Rebel (22.5 mm x 15 mm). Because this sensor covers a smaller area (small-format sensor) than a 35mm film frame, it records a narrower field of view than a 35mm film camera. To help photographers who are used to working with 35mm SLRs visualize the narrower field of view, a magnification factor of 1.6 is applied to the lens' focal length. Thus, on the 20D, a 200mm lens will have a field of view similar to that of a 320mm lens on a 35mm camera. Remember, the focal length doesn't change, just the view seen by the 20D's sensor.

This magnification factor is great for telephoto advocates. However, it causes a problem at the wide-angle end, where a 28mm lens now acts like a 45mm lens on a 35mm camera. A fairly wide lens loses most of its wide-angle capabilities.

Wide angles of view can be difficult to get with small-format sensors. The 20D does accept Canon EF-S lenses, which are specially designed just for this format. They include a 10–22mm zoom that offers an equivalent 16–35mm focal length.

Though small-format, the sensor in the 20D demonstrates improvements in sensor technology. It adds nearly a third more pixels, so obviously each pixel has to be smaller. In the past, this would have meant problems with noise and sensitivity. However, this sensor's 8.2 megapixels offer the same ISO range as the EOS 10D (6.3-megapixel sensor), yet yield less noise while possessing a higher dynamic range.

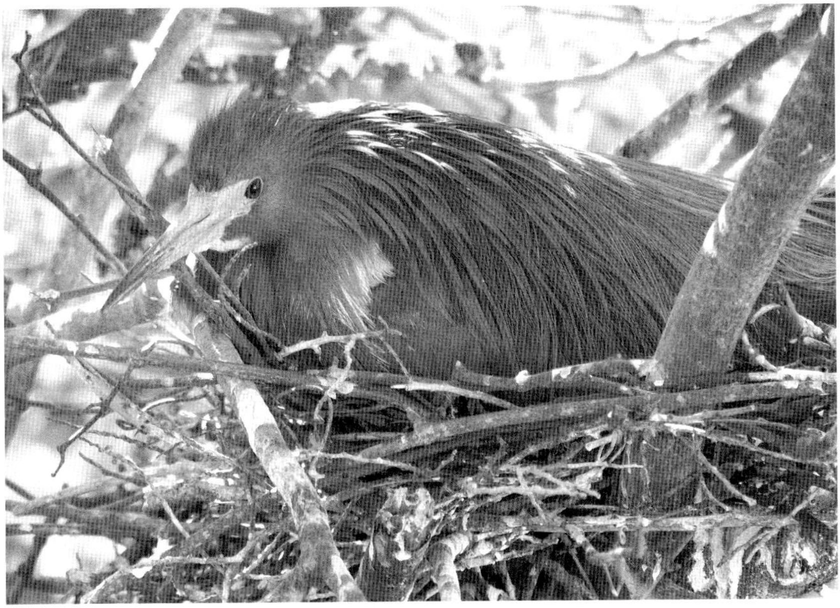

Because the 20D's sensor is smaller than the frame size of 35mm film, a lens' effective focal length is magnified by 1.6x, making telephoto lenses seem more powerful than on a 35mm camera.

Low noise characteristics are extremely important to advanced amateur and professional photographers who want the highest possible image quality. The 20D gives an extraordinarily clean image with exceptional tonalities and the ability to be enlarged with superior results.

Several other things contribute to this improved imaging quality. Canon has worked hard on the design and production of their sensors. They have developed a special on-chip RGB primary filter with larger micro-lenses that reduce the gaps between pixels. This increases the light to each sensor element, resulting in more image signal and less noise. In addition, the camera has a low-noise, high-speed output amplifier as well as power saving circuitry that also reduces noise.

With such low noise, the sensor offers more range and flexibility in sensitivity settings. ISO settings range from 100–1600 in 1/3-stop increments. An extra choice of 3200 can be accessed in Custom Function 08 in the Set-up Menu. While the higher settings do exhibit more noise than the lower settings, even 1600 and 3200 offer remarkable quality considering the speed. Such high settings serve as well as they do because of the intensive work Canon put into the design and production of their sensors.

The on-chip RGB primary color filter uses a standard Bayer pattern over the sensor elements. This is an alternating arrangement of color with 50% green, 25% red, and 25% blue—full color is interpolated from this data. In addition, an infrared cut-off, low-pass filter is located in front of the sensor. This three-layer filter is designed to prevent the false colors and the wavy or rippled look of surfaces (moiré) that can occur when photographing small, patterned areas with high-resolution digital cameras.

Cleaning the Sensor

The EOS 20D does allow you to clean the sensor, but there are precautions to be taken. You must do this carefully and gently, indoors and out of the wind. Your battery must be fully charged so it doesn't fail during cleaning, or you can use the AC adapter. The sensor is very sensitive, so if the gentle cleaning described below doesn't work, you should send the camera to a Canon Service Center for a thorough cleaning.

To clean the sensor, turn the camera on and go to the Set-up Menu. Scroll down using the Quick Control Dial until *Sensor clean* is highlighted. Press the SET button and you will get a new screen—now just follow the instructions. You'll be given *OK* and *Cancel* options. Select *OK* and the LCD Monitor turns off, the mirror will lock up, and the shutter will open. Take the lens off. Then, holding the camera face down (not face up as seen in the manual), use a blower to gently blow any dust or other debris off the bottom of the lens opening first, then off the sensor. Do not use brushes or compressed air because these can damage the sensor's surface. Turn the camera off when done. The mirror and shutter will return to normal. Put the lens back on.

Caution: Never leave a digital SLR without a body cap for any length of time. Lenses should be capped when not in use and rear caps should always be used when a lens is not mounted. These practices will help to prevent dust from reaching the sensor.

Note: Canon specifically recommends against any cleaning techniques or devices that touch the surface of the imaging sensor.

Mirror Lockup

For really critical work on a tripod, such as shooting long exposures or working with macro and super telephoto lenses, sharpness is improved by eliminating the vibrations caused by mirror movement. This is accomplished by locking up the mirror in advance using the EOS 20D's Mirror Lockup function. However, it does mean the viewfinder will be blacked out and the only available drive mode will be single shot (no matter what you have set).

This feature is set with Custom Function 12 (although it will be cancelled automatically after 30 seconds). Once set, you press the Shutter button and the mirror will lock up. Press the Shutter button again to make the exposure. Use a remote switch or the self-timer to keep all movement to a minimum. This is a good use of the self-timer—the shutter will go off two seconds after the mirror is locked up, allowing vibrations to dampen. The self-timer does not work when Bulb Exposure and Mirror Lockup are used together.

Memory cards come in a variety of styles and file capacities. Unlike some digital cameras, the 20D can accept high-capacity CF cards of 2GB and more.

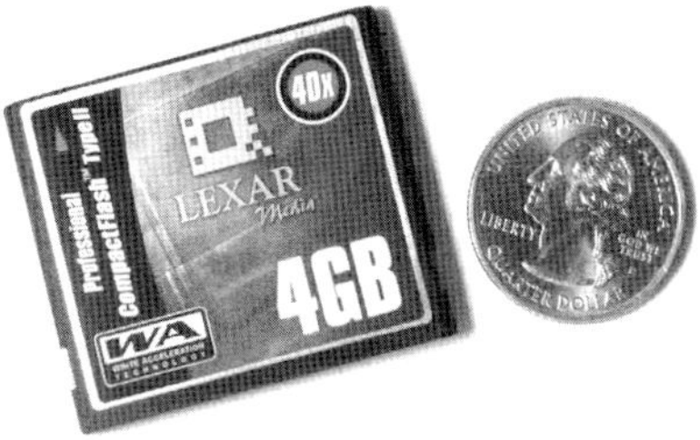

Memory Cards

The Canon EOS 20D uses CompactFlash (CF) memory cards. These cards are a standard in the industry and readily available at most stores carrying digital cameras. You will need a sizeable card to handle the image files of this camera; anything less than a 256 MB card will fill up too quickly (see page 71-75 for specifics). Memory cards are very sturdy, durable devices. They are not damaged by airport security X-rays, nor are they hurt if you drop them or they fall into the water. However, heat will damage them.

To remove the memory card from your camera, simply open the Card Slot Cover on the right side of the camera and push the Card Eject button. It is a good idea to turn the camera off before doing this, even though the 20D will automatically shut itself off when the memory card door is opened. The habit of turning the camera off will let it finish recording to the card. If you should open the Card Slot and remove the card before the camera has written a set of files to it, there is a good possibility you will corrupt the directory or damage the card, making the files impossible to read.

You have a choice in how the camera deals with numbering the images on the card. The numbers can go continuously from 0001 to 9999 even when you change cards, or the camera can reset numbers every time you make a change. The camera automatically creates folders that hold a sequence of 100 numbers (if you erase images as you go, the folder may hold less than 100 files, but the camera will still start a new folder at every 100 numbers). There is no arbitrary advantage to either method of numbering, it is a personal preference depending on your workflow needs.

Continuous numbers can make it easy to track image files over a time period. Resetting numbers will let you organize a shoot by using different CF cards. Folders will go up to 999. At 999, you will get a message (Folder number full) on the LCD Monitor. Once image 9999 is recorded, you will get a message, "Err CF." At that point you have to replace the CF card (formatting it would also work, but then you would lose your images).

Formatting Your Memory Card

Caution: Formatting will erase all images and information stored on the card, including protected images. Be sure that you do not need anything on the card to be saved before you format. (Transfer important images to a computer or other downloading device before formatting the card.)

Before you use a memory card in your camera, it helps to format it specifically for the 20D. To do so, go to the Set-up Menu, then scroll to *Format* using the Quick Control Dial. Press the SET button and the Format menu will appear on the LCD Monitor. It will tell you how much of the card is presently used with images and how big the card is. Use the Quick Control Dial to move the choice to *OK*, press the SET button, and formatting will occur. You will see a screen showing the progress of the formatting. Keep in mind that formatting will erase all of the images on the card, whether they were previously protected or not!

Note: Formatting your CF card once in a while is a good idea to clean your memory card and keep its data structure organized. However, you should never format the card in a computer because it uses different file structures than digital cameras—this can make the card unreadable for the camera.

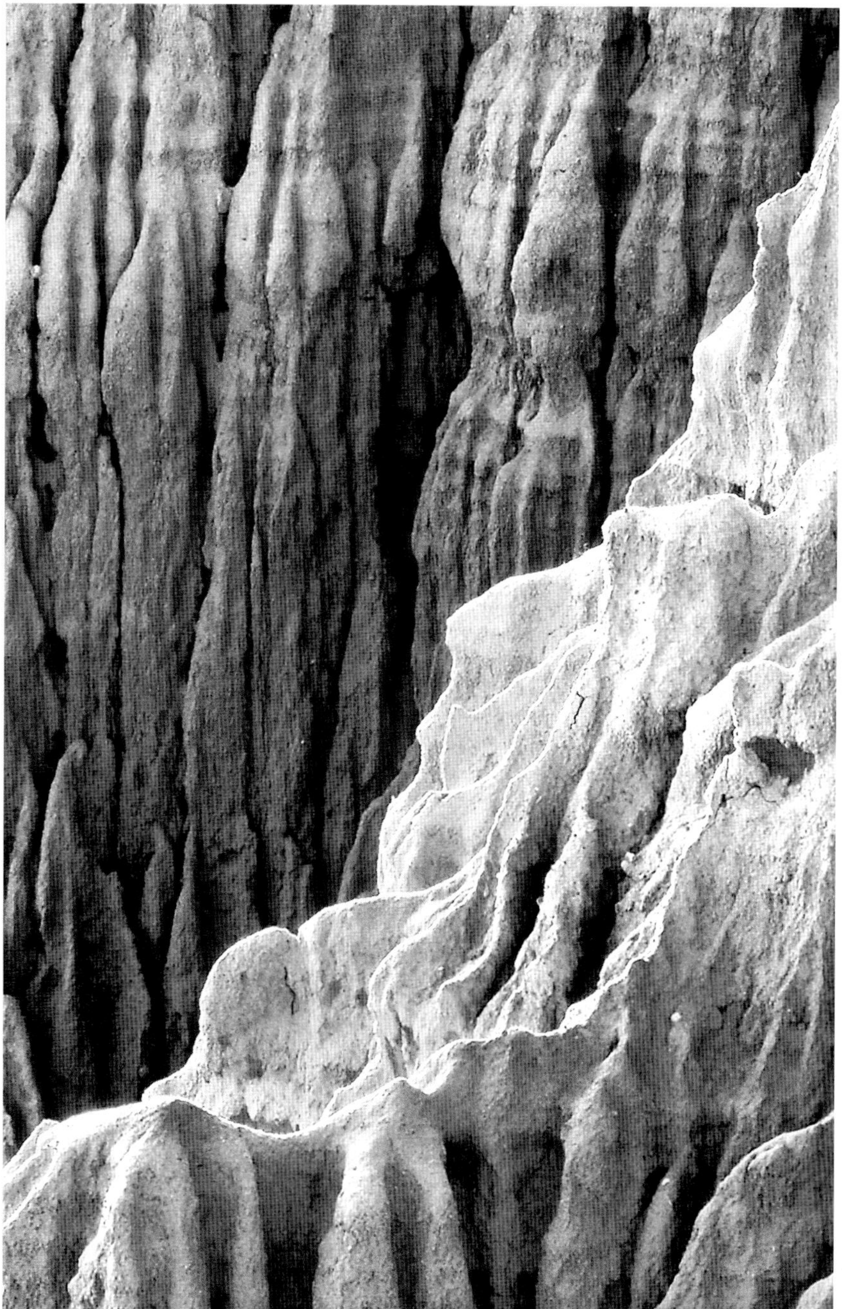

Cleaning the Camera

It is important to keep your camera clean in order to minimize the amount of dirt or dust that could reach the sensor. A good kit of cleaning materials should include the following: a soft camel hair brush to clean off the camera, an antistatic brush and micro-fiber cloth for cleaning the lens, a pack towel for drying the camera in damp conditions (available at outdoor stores), and a small rubber bulb to blow off debris from the lens and the camera (you can get these from a camera store, or use a baby's ear-syringe or an enema bulb—they both work very well).

Always blow and brush debris from the camera before rubbing with any cloth. For lens cleaning, blow and brush first, then clean with a micro-fiber cloth. If you find there is residue on the lens that is hard to remove, you can use a lens cleaning fluid (be sure it is made for camera lenses). Never apply the fluid directly to the lens, as it can seep behind the lens elements and get inside the body of the lens. Apply with a cotton swab, or just spray the edge of your micro-fiber cloth. Rub gently to remove the dirt, then buff the lens with a dry part of the cloth. Replace the cloth in its protective packet to keep it clean. You can wash it in the washing machine (and dry it in the dryer) when it gets dirty.

You don't need to be obsessive about cleaning your camera, just remember that a clean camera and lens helps to ensure that you don't have image problems. Dirt and other residue on the camera can get inside when changing lenses, which causes a problem if it ends up on the sensor. Dust on the sensor will show up as small, dark, out-of-focus spots in the photo (most noticeable in light areas, such as sky). You can minimize problems with sensor dust if you turn the camera off when changing lenses (that keeps static charge from building up), as well as by keeping a body cap on the camera and lens caps on lenses when not in use.

Keeping dust and dirt away from your sensor is critical when using a digital camera. In dry and dusty scenic conditions, be especially careful when changing lenses.

Getting Started in 10 Basic Steps

There are ten things you should check in order to make your work with the camera easier from the start. These steps are especially useful if you have not yet become familiar with the camera. You will probably modify them with experience.

1. Set the 'Auto power off' for a reasonable time. The camera comes with a very short power-off setting of one minute. I guarantee this will frustrate you when the camera has turned itself off just as you are ready to shoot. Perhaps it is more realistic to try four minutes. Change this time period in the Set-up menu. (See page 39)

2. Adjust the eyepiece**:** Use the Dioptric Adjustment knob to the right of the viewfinder to make the focus through your eyepiece as sharp as possible. You can adjust it with a fingertip. I think it is easiest to adjust when the camera is on. Lightly press the Shutter button to display Viewfinder information. Focus on the AF points and on the letters in the Viewfinder information. Never try to make this adjustment by focusing on a scene that is imaged by the lens. (See page 34)

3. Turn on Quick Control Dial**:** This is the big dial on the back of the camera. It will help you control a number of adjustments. To turn it on, move the Power switch (below and to the left of the Quick Control Dial) to a position above ON, to point at a symbol that looks like an angled line. (See page 30)

4. Choose an image size of L(JPEG) or RAW**:** This determines your image file quality. You choose this at the top of the Shooting menu, and turn the Quick Control Dial to select your desired image size. (See page 71)

5. Set your preferred exposure mode**:** Select P, Av, Tv, or M, or any of the preset modes, by using the Mode Dial on the top left of the camera. (See page 111-117)

***6. Choose drive and AF mode*:** Drive is selected by pressing the DRIVE•ISO button located on top of the camera in front of the LCD Panel, then turning the Main Dial (top right front of camera behind Shutter button) to highlight your choice in the LCD Panel. AF is set by pressing the AF-WB button (located on top of camera in front of the LCD Panel) and using the Main Dial to choose an appropriate mode, which appears in the LCD Panel. A good place to start on this camera is AI Servo AF. (See page 98)

***7. Select white balance*:** Auto AWB is a good place to start because the 20D is designed to generally do well with it. To set, press the AF•WB button (on top of the camera in front of the LCD Panel) and rotate the Quick Control Dial—the different white balance choices will display in the LCD Panel. (See page 59)

***8. Pick an ISO setting*:** With the 20D, you can get away with higher settings than usual with other digital cameras. Anything between 100 and 400 will work beautifully. Press the DRIVE•ISO button and turn the Quick Control Dial to see the choices for ISO speed displayed in the LCD Panel. (See page 102)

***9. Set vertical display*:** Choose the *Auto rotate* option in the Set-up menu, then choose *On*. This makes all images appear with correct orientation on the LCD Monitor. If you don't like this, turn the feature off. (See page 83)

***10. Set camera for reasonable review time*:** This camera, like many digital cameras, comes with a default review time (the period of time the picture is displayed on the LCD Monitor after taking the photo) that that is quite short, in this case it is merely two seconds. That's not enough time to analyze anything. I recommend the eight-second setting, which you can always cancel by pressing the shutter release. If you are worried about using too much battery power, just turn off the review function altogether. Go to the Playback menu to change the review time. (See page 80)

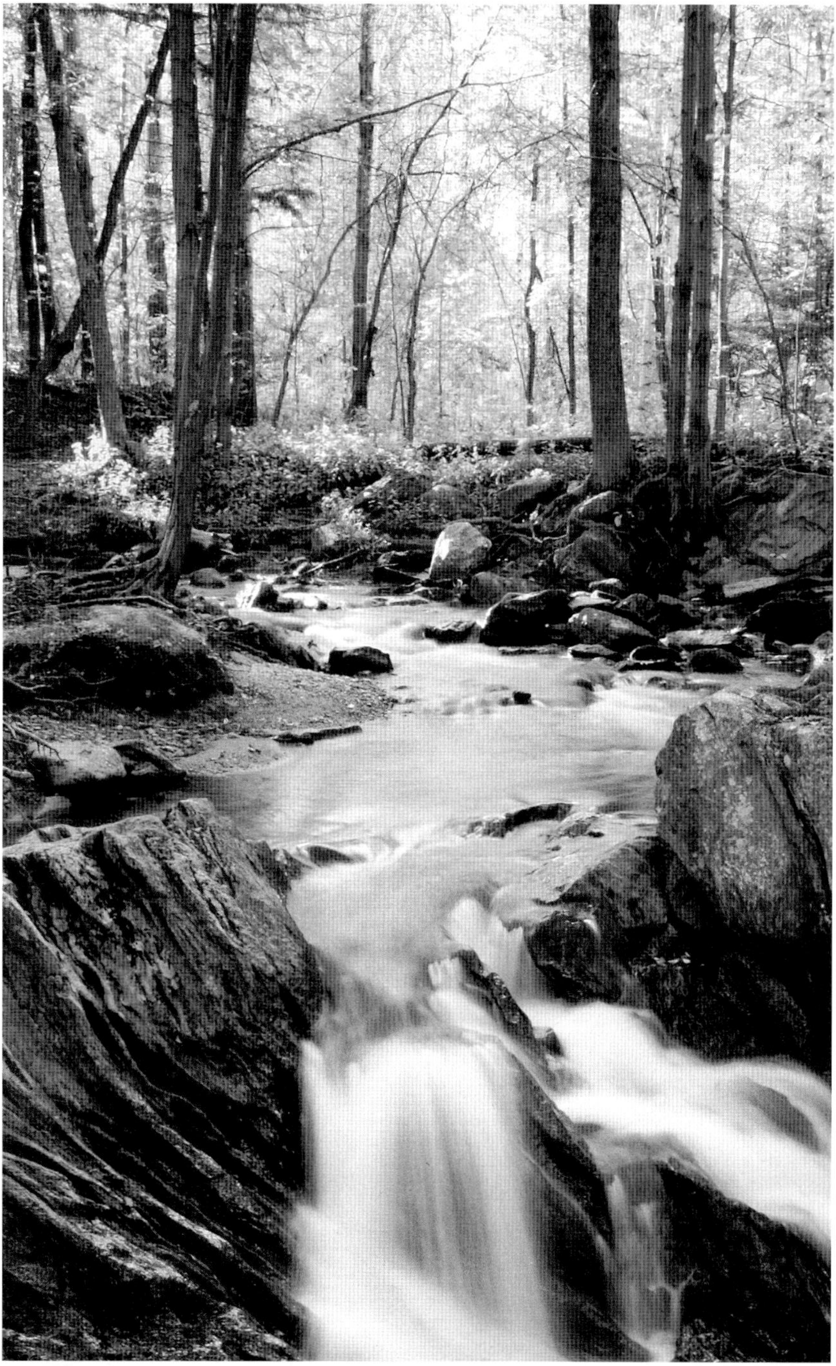

Quick Menu Lookup

Quality, Red-eye On/Off, Beep, Shoot w/o card, AEB (Auto Exposure Bracketing), WB SHIFT/BKT (White balance shift / bracketing), Custom WB, Color temp., Color Space, Parameters

Protect, Rotate, Print order, Auto Play, Review time

Auto power off, Auto rotate, LCD brightness, Date/Time, File numbering, Language, Video system, Communication, Format card, Custom Functions, Clear settings, Sensor cleaning, Firmware Ver.

Custom Functions

1. SET button function
- No function
- Quality
- Parameter
- Menu
- Image replay

2. Long exposure noise reduction (Off, On)
3. Flash sync speed in Av mode (Auto, 1/250)
4. Shutter button/AE lock button
- AF/AE lock
- AE lock/AF
- AF/AF lock, no AE lock
- AE/AF, no AE lock

5. AF-assist beam (emits, does not emit, only ext. flash emits)
6. Exposure level increments (1/3 stop, 1/2 stop)
7. Flash firing (Fires, does not fire)
8. ISO expansion (Off, On)
9. Bracket Sequence / Auto cancel
- 0, -, + / Enable
- 0, -, + / Disable
- -, 0, + / Enable
- -, 0, + / Disable

10. AF Point - Superimposed display (On, Off)
11. Menu button display position
- Previous (top in power off)
- Previous
- Top

12. Mirror lockup (Disable, Enable)
13. AF point selection method
- Normal
- Multi-controller direct
- Quick Control Dial direct

14. E-TTL II (Evaluative, Average)
15. Shutter curtain sync (1st curtain, 2nd curtain)
16. Safety Shift in Av or Tv (Disable, Enable)
17. Lens AF stop button function
- AF stop
- AF start
- AE lock while metering
- AF point: M-> Auto / Auto -> ctr.
- One Shot <-> AI Servo
- IS start

18. Add original decision data (Off, On)

Troubleshooting

Error Codes

- **Err 01**

Communication problem between camera and lens. Clean contacts

- **Err 02**

Problem with CF card. Remove and re-insert, reformat, or try a different card.

- **Err 04**

CF card is full. Delete unneeded images or switch cards.

- **Err 05**

Pop up flash problem. Make sure nothing is preventing the flash from deploying. Turn camera off and on.

- **Err CF**

Problem with CF card. Card may have reached maximum/file number (9999). Switch cards or reformat.

- **Err 99**

Miscellaneous error. May occur with use of non-Canon lens. Remove and re-install the battery.

Magic Lantern Guides

Canon EOS 20D Quick Reference Card

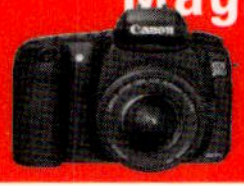

Focus

• ***Set focus mode***
Press AF-WB use

• ***One Shot***
When shutter is pressed half way, stops and locks when focus is achieved

• ***AI Focus AF***
Switches between One Shot and Servo

• ***AI Servo AF***
Tracks subject and focuses continuously until exposure

• ***Selecting AF Point***
Press AF-WB, then use or or to select AF Point

• ***Reset AF Point***
Push in the same direction of the current focus point to return to automatic AF point selection

Exposure

• ***Set metering mode***
Press use

• ***Evaluative Metering***
Measures all metering zones across image – emphasizing AF point

• ***Partial Metering***
Measures 9% of frame – emphasizing center of image; with telephoto, similar to spot meter

• ***Center-weighted Averaged Metering***
Measures an average reading across the center of horizontal frame

• ***Selecting ISO***
Press DRIVE-ISO, use to select

White Balance

• ***Set White Balance mode***
Press AF-WB, use to select mode

• ***Custom White Balance***
Shoot reference image; use Custom WB to select reference image, then press AF-WB and use to select

• ***Set White Balance by color temperature***
Press AF-WB, use to select ; use Color temp to select (degrees) Kelvin

Overrides

***Exposure lock** (AE Lock)*
Lock the exposure setting by pressing the * button

Exposure Compensation
Override the auto exposure in increments of 1/2 or 1/3 stops by setting the switch to and using to adjust compensation

Flash Exposure Compensation
Set flash exposure compensation +/- 2 stops in 1/2 or 1/3 stop increments. Press , use to select compensation

Autoexposure Bracketing
Bracket exposure by up to +/- 2 stops. In select AEB and use to adjust -- set DRIVE-ISO to to take 3 shots automatically

White Balance Correction and Bracketing
Adjust color balance in two axes. In , select WB Shift/BK. For white balance correction, use ; to turn on color bracketing, use or

Processing Parameters

Parameter 1
Crisp, sharp and vivid. One setting above normal on Contrast, Sharpness and Color Saturation.

Parameter 2
Natural. All controls set for normal

Set1, Set2, Set3
Custom settings for Contrast, Sharpness, Saturation and Color tone.

B/W
Ye:Yellow—Darkens skies, more natural looking black and white
R:Red—Dramatic; reds become lighter, blues become darker
Or:Orange—Midway between effect of yellow and red
G:Green—Makes Caucasian skin tones more natural

In-Camera Processing and File Formats

There has been a mistaken notion that JPEG is a file format for amateur photographers while RAW is a format for professionals. This is really not the case. Pros use JPEG and amateurs can use RAW (technically, JPEG is a compression scheme and not a format, but the term is commonly used to denote format and that is how we will use it).

There is no question that RAW offers some distinct benefits for the photographer who needs them, including the ability to make greater changes to the image file before the image degrades from over processing. The 20D's RAW format (called CR2 and originally developed by Canon for the EOS-1D Mark II) includes revised processing benefits to make it more flexible and versatile for photographers than previous versions. It can also handle more metadata and store processing parameters for future use.

However, RAW is not for everyone. It requires more work and more time to process than other formats. For the photographer who likes to work quickly and wants to spend less time at the computer, JPEG may offer distinct advantages and, with the 20D, even give better results. This might sound radical considering what some "experts" say about RAW in relation to JPEG, but I suspect they have never shot an image with an EOS 20D set for high-quality JPEG capture.

The ability to shoot RAW files offers processing benefits to photographers, such as increased flexibility with exposure and white balance. However, RAW files do require more computer processing time.

The reason the 20D delivers such exceptional images using JPEG is because of Canon's unique DIGIC Imaging Engine (DIGIC for short). Canon has long had exceptionally strong in-camera processing capabilities, and this newest version of their high-performance processor, called DIGIC II, builds on the technology from previous Canon processors.

DIGIC II intelligently translates the image signal as it comes from the sensor, optimizing that signal as it is converted into digital data. In essence, it is like having your own computer expert making the best possible adjustments as it processes the captured RAW data file for you. It works on the image in-camera after the shutter is clicked and before the image is recorded to the memory card, improving color balance—reducing noise, refining tonalities in the brightest areas, and more. In these ways it has the potential to make JPEG files superior to unprocessed RAW files, reducing the need for RAW processing.

It is amazing that the DIGIC II handles data so fast that it does not impede camera speed. There is a single chip in the 20D with four-channel signal reading and image data processing that is appreciably faster than earlier units. Color reproduction of highly saturated, bright objects is also much improved. Auto white balance is better, especially at low color temperatures (such as tungsten light). In addition, false colors and noise, which have always challenged digital capture, have been reduced (and this is something that RAW files cannot offer).

DIGIC II also affects the 20D's ability to write image data to the memory card in both JPEG and RAW. Write speed is now faster, enabling the camera to take advantage of the benefit offered by high-speed memory cards. It is important to understand that this does not affect how quickly the camera can take pictures. Rather, it affects how fast it can transfer images from its buffer to the card. It won't change the shots per second, but it will affect how many images can be taken in succession.

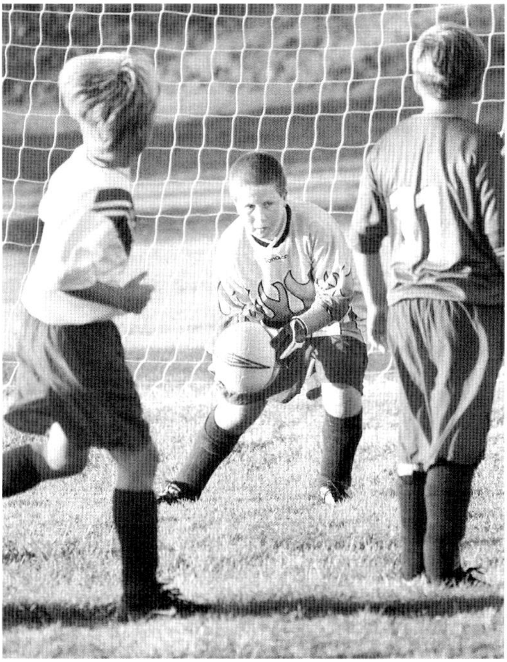

The 20D can shoot five frames per second, which increases your chances of getting exactly the action shot you want.

Speed

There are factors, however, that do affect how many shots per second the camera can take. Having a high-megapixel sensor with its comparatively large amount of data has usually meant a slower camera. Yet this is not true of the 20D. It can take pictures at a speedy 5 frames per second (fps). Even at maximum resolution, the camera has a burst duration of 23 JPEG or 6 RAW frames (this will occur only with the fastest memory cards). It is even designed to keep up with autofocus. The camera itself has very fast response times: 0.2-second startup, 65-millisecond (ms) lag time for shutter release, and finder blackout (when the mirror is up during exposure) of only 115 ms (due to a new high-speed mirror drive). No camera in its class could match these times when the 20D was introduced.

During continuous shooting, each image is placed into a buffer (special temporary memory in the camera) before it is recorded to the memory card. The faster the memory card, the faster the buffer will be emptied, allowing more images to be taken in sequence. If the buffer becomes full, the camera will stop shooting until the card writing can catch up. You will then see a *buSY* message on the LCD Panel and in the viewfinder.

Processing Parameters

In addition to the optimizing technology of DIGIC II, you can choose specific ways in which the camera will perform further image processing. This can be especially helpful if you are printing image files directly from the camera without using a computer, or when you need to supply a particular type of image to a client.

You gain access to these Processing Parameters through the Shooting menu (press MENU button, scroll with the Quick Control Dial to *Parameters,* then press the SET button—you will use the Quick Control Dial and SET button to further scroll and select among the different parameter options and sub options). To return to the Shooting menu screen at any time, press the MENU button again.

All of the Processing Parameters (except B/W) control the degree of processing applied to four aspects of an image: *Contrast, Sharpness, Saturation,* and *Color tone.* These are menu choices, and are represented by a selection point on a slider-type scale. For B/W (black-and-white), parameters for *Filter effect* and *Toning effect* are added, while the color effects, *Saturation* and *Color tone,* are removed.

Contrast will increase or decrease the contrast of the scene that is captured by the camera. *Sharpness* refers to the amount of sharpening that is applied to the image file by the camera. *Saturation* influences color richness or intensity. *Color tone* helps the photographer decide how red or how yellow to render skin tones, but will also affect other colors as well.

The different settings for these in-camera parameters are:

- ***Parameter 1***—Automatically determined by the camera and cannot be changed, giving a set value for *Contrast, Sharpness,* and *Color saturation* that is one step higher than midpoint. This setting has no affect on *Color tone.* It gives a vivid and crisp image file and is the only setting used for the Basic Zone modes. It is designed for direct printing from the camera.

- ***Parameter 2***—Default for the Creative Zone modes and automatically selects the value for each of the parameter choices at the midpoint of their ranges. It renders a natural, or less intense, look for images that will be displayed on the computer. Like *Parameter 1,* this setting cannot be changed by the user.

- ***Set 1, Set 2, and Set 3***—Each allows you to create and register a different set of parameters that you can apply to image files to meet specific photographic needs. Each setting is flexible; you can use the Quick Control Dial to move the selector to the left or right (minus or plus) of the midpoint for *Contrast, Sharpness, Saturation,* and *Color tone.*

While specific situations may affect where you place your control points for the these flexible options, here are suggestions to consider:

- ***Create a hazy or cloudy day setting***—Make one of the parameter sets capture more contrast and color on days where contrast and color are weak. Increase the scale for *Contrast* and *Color saturation* by one or two points (experiment to see what you like when you open the files on your computer or use the camera for direct printing). You can also increase the red setting of *Color tone* (adjust the scale to the left).

- ***Create a portrait setting***—Make a set that favors skin tones, reducing contrast by one point while increasing saturation by one point (this is very subjective—some photographers may prefer less saturation) and warming skin tones (by moving *Color tone* toward the red, or left side) by one point.

- ***Create a Velvia (an intensely colored slide film) look***—Increase *Contrast* two points, *Sharpness* one point, and *Saturation* by two points.

Finally there is one more valuable parameter control in the 20D:

- ***B/W***—The last of the settings for Processing Parameters, this allows you to record pure black-and-white images to the memory card, a feature unique at this point to this digital SLR. (Some compact digital cameras do include a black-and-white setting, but none have the controls that are available on the 20D.) *Contrast* and *Sharpness* are the same adjustments as used with the other settings. In addition, there are *Filter effect* and *Toning effect*.

The parameters for *Filter effect* offer four tonal effects that mimic what different colored filters do with black-and-white film. A fifth setting, *N:None*, means no filter effects are applied. Each color choice in the *Filter effect* menu will make colors similar to your color selection look lighter, and colors opposite it on the color wheel will record darker.

Ye:Yellow is a modest effect that darkens skies slightly and gives what many black-and-white aficionados consider the most natural looking of black-and-white filters. *Or:Orange* is next in intensity, but is better explained if you understand the use of red. *R:Red* is dramatic, making rather light anything that is red, such as flowers or ruddy skin tones, while blues become dark. Skies turn quite striking and sunlit scenes gain in contrast (the sunny areas are warm-toned and the shadows are cool-toned, so the warms get lighter and the cools get darker). *Or:Orange* is in-between yellow and red. The last filter effect is *G:Green*. This makes Caucasian skin tones look

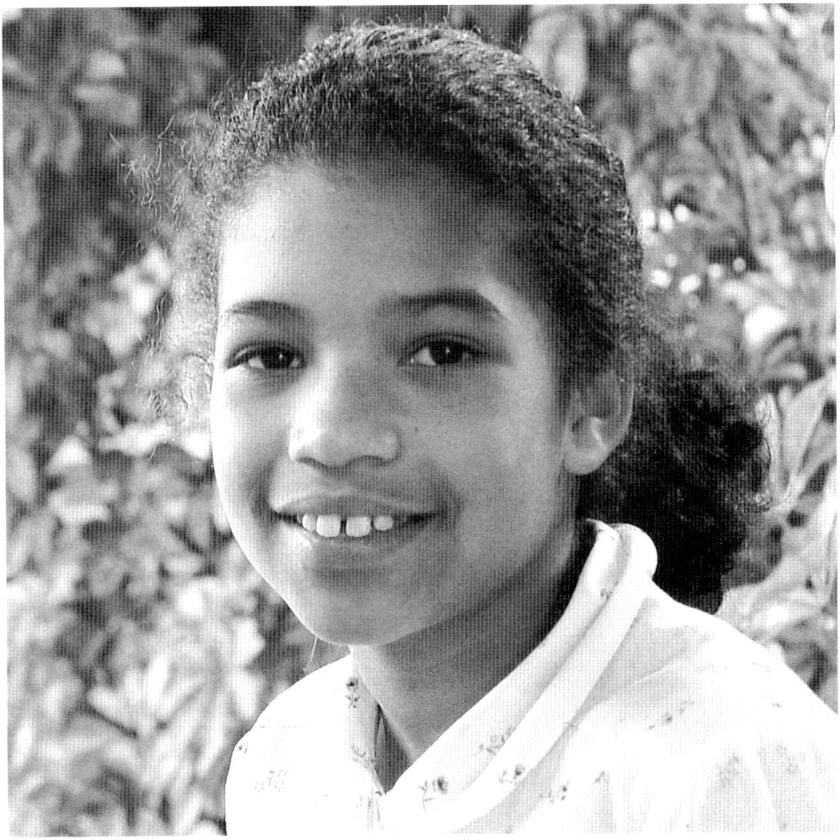

You can program the 20D to create settings for image processing, called parameters. Among other possibilities, you can consistently enhance portraits of family and friends.

more natural and foliage gets bright and lively in tone. Of course, the great thing about digital is that if you aren't sure what any of these do, you can take the picture and see the effect immediately on the LCD Monitor.

Toning effect adds color to the black-and-white image so it looks like a toned black-and-white print. Your choices include *N:None, S:Sepia, B:Blue, P:Purple,* and *G:Green*. Sepia and blue are the tones we are most used to seeing in such prints.

White Balance

White balance is an important digital camera control. It addresses a problem that has plagued film photographers for ages: how to deal with the different color temperatures of various light sources. While color adjustments can be made in the computer after shooting, especially when shooting RAW, there is a definite benefit to setting white balance properly from the start. The 20D helps you do this with an improved Auto white balance setting AWB that makes colors more accurate and natural than earlier digital SLRs. In addition, improved algorithms and the DIGIC II processor make Auto white balance more stable as you shoot a scene from different angles and focal lengths (which is always a challenge when using automatic white balance). Further, white balance has been improved to make color reproduction more accurate under low lights.

While Auto will give excellent results in a number of situations, many photographers find they prefer the control offered by presets and custom settings. With nine separate white balance settings, plus white balance compensation and bracketing, the ability to carefully control color balance is greatly enhanced in the 20D. It is well worth the effort to learn how to use the different white balance functions so that you can get the best color with the most efficient workflow in all situations (including RAW). This is especially important in strongly colored scenes, such as sunrise or sunset, which can fool Auto white balance.

The basic settings are simple enough to learn that they should become part of the photography decision-making process (however, they can only be used with the Creative Zone exposure modes, see page 111). The more involved setting for Custom white balance 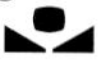 is also a valuable tool to understand and use for rendering the truest color in all conditions.

Set white balance by pressing the AF•WB button on the top right of the camera (you don't have to hold it down). Then rotate the Quick Control Dial to select the desired icon from the LCD Panel.

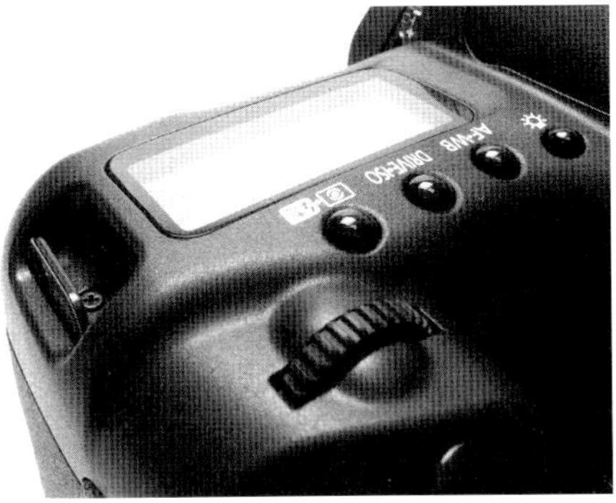

Depressing the AF•WB button activates the Quick Control Dial for six seconds. Turn this Dial to select the desired white balance settings.

Camera Settings

AWB **Auto: Color temperature range of approximately 3000 – 7000K**

This setting examines the scene for you, interprets the light it sees (in the range denoted above) using the DIGIC II processor (even with RAW), compares the conditions to what the engineers have determined works for such readings, and sets a white balance to make colors look neutral (i.e., whites appear pure, without color casts, and skin tones appear normal).

Auto can be a useful setting when you are moving quickly from one type of light to another, or whenever you hope to get neutral colors and need to shoot fast. Even if it isn't the perfect setting for all conditions, it will often get you close enough so that only a little adjustment is needed later using your image-editing software. However, if you have time, it is often better to choose from the white balance settings listed below, because colors will be more consistent from picture to picture. While Auto is well-designed, it can only interpret how it "thinks" a scene should look, so if your wide-angle and telephoto shots of the same subject change what is seen by the camera in terms of colors, the camera will readjust for each shot, often resulting in inconsistent color from shot to shot.

Daylight: Approximately 5200K
This setting adjusts the camera to make colors appear natural when shooting in sunlit situations between about 10 A.M. and 4 P.M. (middle of the day). At other times, when the sun is lower in the sky and has more red light, the scenes photographed using this setting will appear warmer than normally seen with our eyes. It makes indoor scenes under incandescent lights look very warm indeed.

Shade: Approximately 7000K
Shadowed subjects under blue skies can end up very bluish in tone, so this setting warms the light to make colors look natural, without any blue color cast (at least that's the ideal—individual situations will affect how effectively the setting performs). The Shade setting is a good one to use anytime you want to warm up a scene (especially when people are included), but you have to experiment to see how you like this creative use of the setting.

Cloudy: Approximately 6000K
Even though the symbol for this setting is a cloud, its full name is actually the **Cloudy/twilight/sunset** setting. It warms up cloudy scenes as if you had a warming filter, making sunlight appear warm, but not quite to the degree that the Shade setting does. You may prefer the Cloudy setting to Shade when shooting people since the effect is not as strong. Both settings actually work well for sunrise and sunset, giving the warm colors that we expect to see in such photographs. However, the Cloudy setting offers a slightly weaker effect. You really do have to experiment a bit when using these settings for creative effect. Make the final comparisons on the computer.

Tungsten Light: Approximately 3200K
Tungsten Light is designed to give natural results with quartz lights (generally balanced to 3200K). It also reduces the strong orange color that is typical when photographing lamp-lit indoor scenes with daylight balanced settings. Since this control adds a cold tone to other conditions, it can also be used creatively for this purpose (to make a snow scene bluer, for example).

White Fluorescent Light: Approximately 4000K

The Auto setting often works well with fluorescents but, under many conditions, the White Fluorescent Light setting is more precise and predictable. Fluorescent lights usually appear green in photographs, so this setting adds magenta to neutralize that effect. (Since fluorescents can be extremely variable, and since the 20D has only one fluorescent choice, you may find that precise color can only be achieved with the Custom white balance setting.) You can also use this setting creatively anytime you wish to add a pinkish warm tone to your photo (such as during sunrise or sunset).

Flash: Approximately 6000K

Light from flash tends to be a little colder than daylight, so this warms it up. According to Canon tech folks, this setting is essentially the same as Cloudy (the Kelvin temperature is the same); it is simply labeled differently to make it easier to use. I actually use both Flash and Cloudy a lot, finding them to be good, all-around settings that give a slight but attractive warm tone to outdoor scenes.

Custom: Approximately 2000 – 10,000K

A very important tool for the digital photographer, Custom is a setting that even pros often don't fully understand. It is a very precise and adaptable way of getting accurate or creative white balance. It has no specific white balance K temperature, but is set based on a specific neutral tone in the light to be photographed. However, it deals with a significantly wider range than Auto. That can be very useful.

The Custom setting lets you choose a white (or gray) target and has the camera white balance on it. First, while in this setting, take a picture of something white (or a known neutral tone) that is in the same light as your subject. You can use a piece of paper or a gray card. It does not have to be in focus, but it should fill the image area. Be sure the exposure is set to make this object gray to light gray in tone, and not dark (underexposed) or washed out white (overexposed).

Then, go to the Shooting menu, choose *Custom WB* using the Quick Control Dial and push the SET button. The last shot you took (the one for white balance) should be displayed in the LCD Monitor. Otherwise, use the Quick Control Dial to choose the image you shot of the white or gray object. Push SET again and the white balance is adjusted to that shot. A note appears, *"Change WB to Custom WB,"* as a reminder.

Now you can use this registered Custom setting by going to the AF•WB button and choosing the Custom icon  . You have created a new white balance setting that will stay associated with the Custom choice until you repeat this process for a new subject.

The procedure just described produces neutral colors in some very difficult conditions. However, if the lighting is mixed in color, like a situation where the subject is lit on one side by a window and on the other by incandescent lights, you will only get neutral colors for the light that the white card was in. Also, when shooting in reduced spectrum lights, such as sodium vapor, you will not get a neutral white under any white balance setting.

You can also use Custom white balance to create special color for a scene. In this case, you white-balance on a color that is not white or gray. You can use a pale blue, for example, to generate a nice amber color. If you balance on the blue, the camera adjusts the color to neutral, which in essence removes blue, so the scene will have an amber cast. You can use different strengths of blue for varied results. You could use any color you want for white balancing—the camera will work to remove (or reduce) that color, which means the opposite color will become stronger (for example, using a pale magenta will increase the green response).

K **Color Temperature**: **Set Kelvin temperature (2800—10,000K)** This setting offers a wide range of possibilities and is recommended for film photographers experienced in using a color-temperature meter and color-compensation (CC) filters. In addition, it can be used in any situation where you want to warm up or cool down the image. It is a multi-step adjustment. After pressing the AF•WB button and selecting **K** on the LCD Panel using the Quick Control Dial, rotate the Quick Control Dial again to get into the Shooting menu. Then choose *Color Temp.* and press the SET button. Next, turn the Quick Control Dial once more to select your desired color temperature, pressing the SET button to lock-in your choice.

Note: Many photographers use color temperature meters. Unfortunately, various meters do not read color temperature exactly the same. The Kelvin numbers for the 20D's white balance settings are approximate and cannot be precisely related to a different device's color temperature readings.

White Balance Correction

The 20D goes beyond the capabilities of many cameras in offering control over white balance—there is actually a white balance correction feature built into the camera. You might think of this as exposure compensation for white balance. It is like having a set of color balancing filters in four colors (blue, amber, green, and magenta) and in varied strengths. Photographers accustomed to using color conversion or color correction filters will find this feature quite helpful in getting just the right color.

The setting is pretty easy to manage using the Multi-controller . First, go to the Shooting menu, scroll to *WB SHIFT/BKT* with the Quick Control Dial and press the SET button. A menu screen will appear with a graph that has a horizontal axis from blue to amber (left to right) and a vertical axis from green to magenta (top to bottom). You move a selection point within that graph with the Multi-controller. You will see a visual indication on the graph as you change the position of the selection point and, at the same time, an alphanumeric display is visible in the upper right of the screen showing a letter for the color (B,A,G, or M) and a number for the setting. For photographers used to color-balancing filters, each increment of color adjustment equals

5 MIREDS of a color-temperature changing filter (a MIRED is a measuring unit for the strength of a color temperature conversion filter). Remember to set the correction back to zero when conditions change.

White Balance Auto Bracketing

When you run into a difficult lighting situation and want to be sure of the best possible white balance settings, another option is white balance auto bracketing. This is actually quite different than autoexposure bracketing. With the latter, three separate exposures are taken of a scene, whereas with white balance auto bracketing you take just one exposure and the camera processes it to give you three different white balance options.

Note: Using white balance bracketing will slightly delay the recording of images to the memory card. You cannot use white balance bracketing with your image-recording quality set to RAW or RAW+JPEG (see page 73).

This bracketing is done up to +/- 3 levels (again, each step is equal to 5 MIREDS of a color correction filter). You can bracket from blue to amber or from green to magenta. Keep in mind that even at the strongest settings, the color changes will be fairly subtle.

The white balance bracketing will be based on whatever white balance mode you have currently selected. The selected mode's icon will blink to tell you that white balance bracketing is being used. You access white balance bracketing by selecting *WB SHIFT/BKT* in the Shooting menu and pressing the SET button. The graph screen with the horizontal (blue/amber) and vertical (green/magenta) axes will appear on the LCD Monitor. Rotate the Quick Control Dial to adjust the bracketing amount—to the right (clockwise) to set the blue/amber adjustment then back to zero and go to the left (counter clockwise) for green/magenta (press SET after each of the color-scale adjustments). You can also shift your setting from the center point of the graph by using the Multi-controller.

Note: The default for white balance bracketing records an original image at the currently selected white balance setting, then internally creates an additional set of (1) a bluer image and a more amber image, or (2) a magenta and greener image. Use C.FN-09 to change bracketing sequence.

The obvious use of this feature is to deal with tricky lighting conditions. However, it has other uses as well. You may want to add a warm touch to a portrait but are not sure how strong you want it. You could select the Cloudy setting, for example, then use white balance bracketing to get the tone you're looking for (the bracketing will give you the standard Cloudy white-balanced shot, plus versions warmer and cooler than that). Or, you may run into a situation where the light changes from one part of the image to another. Here, you can shoot the bracket then combine the white balance versions using an image-processing program (i.e., take the nicely white-balanced parts of one bracketed photograph and combine them with a different bracketed shot that has good white-balance in the areas that were lacking in the first photo).

RAW and White Balance

Since the RAW format allows you to change white balance "after the shot", some photographers have come to believe that it is not important to select an appropriate white balance at the time the photo is taken. While it is true that Auto white balance and RAW will give excellent results in many situations, this approach can cause consistency and workflow challenges. White balance choice is important because, when you bring CR2 files into software for "translation," the files come up with the settings that you chose during initial image capture. Sure you can edit those settings in the computer, but why not make a good RAW image better by merely tweaking the white balance with minor revisions at the image-processing stage rather than starting from an image that requires major correction? There will be times that getting a good white balance setting is difficult, and this is really when the RAW software white balance correction can be a big help.

EOS 20D Functions

		Basic Zone							Creative Zone				
									P	Tv	Av	M	A-DEP
Quality	JPEG	■	■	■	■	■	■	■	■	■	■	■	■
	RAW								■	■	■	■	■
	RAW + JPEG								■	■	■	■	■
ISO speed	Auto	×	×	×	×	×	×	×					
	Manual								■	■	■	■	■
White balance	Auto WB	×	×	×	×	×	×	×	■	■	■	■	■
	Preset WB, Custom WB, Color Temperature setting, WB correction, WB bracketing								■	■	■	■	■
Parameters		× (Parameter 1)							■	■	■	■	■
AF	One-shot		×	×	×		×		■	■	■	■	×
	AI Servo					×			■	■	■	■	—
	AI Focus	×						×	■	■	■	■	—
	AF point selection: Auto	×	×	×	×	×	×	×	■	■	■	■	×
	AF point selection: Manual								■	■	■	■	
Exposure	Evaluative	×	×	×	×	×	×	×	■	■	■	■	■
	Partial								■	■	■	■	■
	Centerweighted average								■	■	■	■	■
Metering mode	Program shift								■				
	Exposure compensation								■	■	■		■
	AEB								■	■	■	■	■
	AE lock								■	■	■		■
	Depth-of-field preview								■	■	■	■	■
Drive	Single	×		×	×		×	×	■	■	■	■	■
	Continuous		×			×			■	■	■	■	■
Built-in flash	Auto	×	×		×		×						
	Manual								■	■	■	■	■
	Flash off			×		×		×					
	red-eye reduction	■	■		■		■		■	■	■	■	■
	FE lock								■	■	■	■	■
	Flash exposure compensation								■	■	■	■	■
Custom Functions / Clearing all Custom Functions									■	■	■	■	■
Camera setting reset									■	■	■	■	■
Image sensor cleaning									■	■	■	■	■

× = automatically selected by camera
■ = user selected

This chart shows different exposure modes and tells which camera functions are available in each of them. It also illustrates which functions are set automatically by the camera.

File Formats

The Canon EOS 20D records images as either JPEG or RAW files. It is important to understand how the sensor processes an image. It sees a certain range of tones coming to it from the lens. Too much light, and the detail is washed out; too little light, and the picture is dark. This is analog (continuous) information, and it must be converted to digital (which is true for any file format, including RAW or JPEG). The complete data is based on 12-bits of color information, which is changed to 8-bit color data for JPEG, or simply placed virtually unchanged into a 16-bit file for RAW. (A bit is the smallest piece of information that a computer uses—an acronym for binary digit. Data of eight bits or higher are required for true photographic color.) This occurs for each of three different color channels employed by the 20D: red, green, and blue. RAW files have very little processing applied by the camera. The fact that they contain 12-bit color information is a little confusing since this information is put into a file that is actually a 16-bit format.

Both 8-bit and 16-bit files have the same range from pure white to pure black because that range is influenced only by the capability of the sensor. If the sensor cannot capture detail in areas that are too bright or too dark, then a RAW file cannot deliver that detail any better than a JPEG file. It is true that RAW allows greater technical control over an image than JPEG, primarily because it starts with more data (12-bits in a 16-bit file), meaning there are more "steps" of information between the white and black extremes of the sensor's sensitivity range. These steps are especially noticeable in the darkest and lightest areas of the photo. So it appears the RAW file has more exposure latitude and greater adjustment to the image is possible before banding or color tearing becomes noticeable.

JPEG format compresses (or reduces) the size of the image file, allowing more pictures to fit on a memory card. The JPEG algorithms carefully look for redundant data in the file (such as a large area of a single color) and remove it, while keeping instructions on how to reconstruct the file. JPEG is therefore referred to as a "lossy" format because technically, data is lost. The computer will rebuild the lost data quite well as long as the compression is low.

It is essential to note that both RAW and JPEG files can give excellent results. Photographers who shoot both use the flexibility of RAW files to deal with tough exposure situations, and the JPEG file when they need fast and easy handling of images. Which format will work best for you? Your own personal way of shooting and working should dictate that. If you are dealing with problem lighting and colors, for example, RAW will give you a lot of flexibility in controlling them. If you can carefully control your exposures and keep images consistent, JPEG will be more efficient.

RAW Exposure Processing

JPEG processing is easy. You can do it with any image-processing program. However, not all such programs can open RAW files; special software is required to convert from RAW. Canon does supply a dedicated software program with the 20D called EOS Viewer Utility. It is specifically designed for CR2 files and allows you to open and smartly process them. You can also choose other processing programs that make converting from RAW files easier, such as Phase One's C1 software. These independent software programs are intended for professional use and can be expensive. Their advantage tends to be ease-of-use for better processing decisions, although Canon's optional Digital Photo Professional (DPP), a high-level RAW conversion program is quite powerful.

The disadvantage of most RAW conversion programs is that they are not integrated into any image-editing software. This means you have to open and work on your photo, then save it and reopen it in an editing program, such as Adobe Photoshop Elements. Adobe met this challenge by including RAW conversion capabilities in Photoshop CS (there is a RAW plug-in available that works similarly for earlier versions) and in Photoshop Elements 3.0. This means you can open a RAW file directly in either of these programs, do the conversions, and

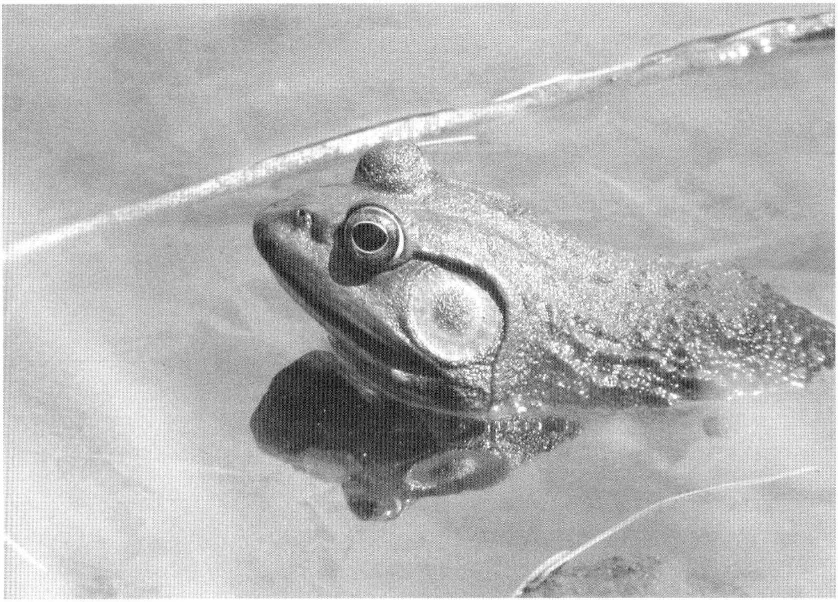

You can shoot in both RAW and JPEG file formats simultaneously, giving either flexibility in difficult lighting situations or the choice to spend less time in post processing. ©Eric Dougherty

then continue to work on the file without leaving the program. You will have to update your Photoshop CS software if you have had it for a while, since the CR2 file-type is a recent one not included in the original CS program (check for updates at www.adobe.com). Workflow is much improved and control over the RAW file is quite good, although some photographers still prefer the conversion algorithms of other programs.

Whatever method you choose to gain access to RAW files in your computer, you will have excellent control over the images in terms of exposure and color of light. There is special metadata (shooting information stored by the camera) in the file containing the exposure settings you selected at the time of shooting—this is used by the RAW conversion program when

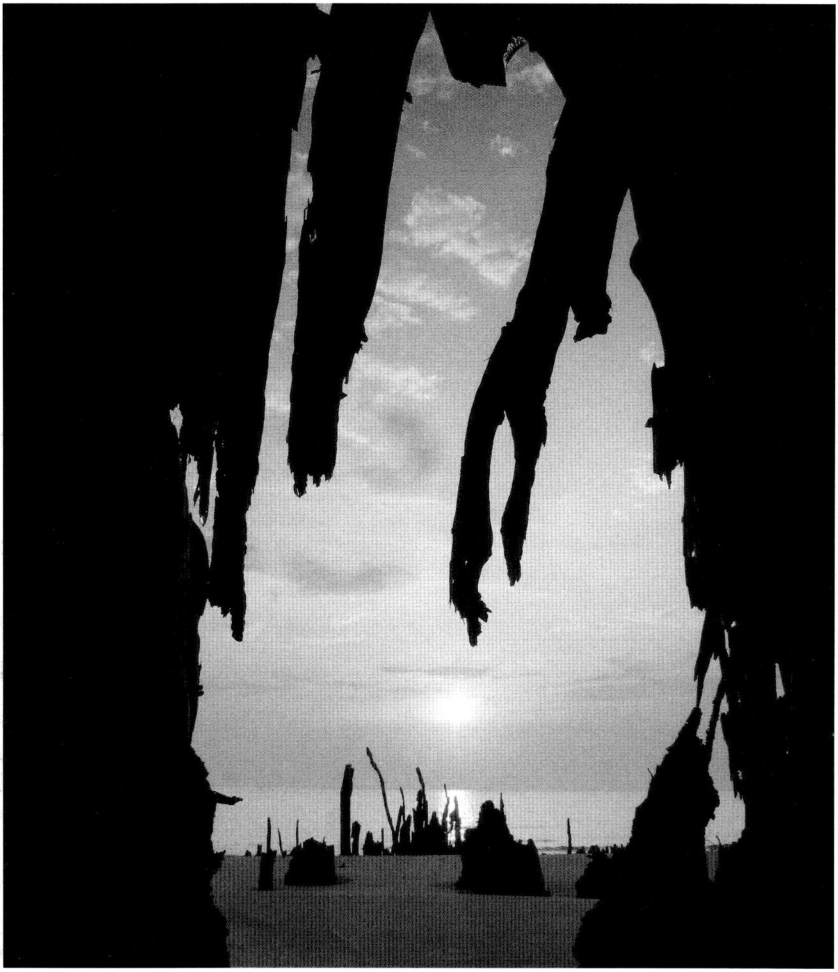

The right software can streamline the RAW conversion process.

it opens an image. You can then change these exposure values without causing harm to the file. Most RAW software allows batch processing. This allows you to adjust a group of photos to specific settings and can be a very important way to deal with multiple photos from the same shoot.

Improved RAW Conversion Software

While RAW can be important for many photographers, Canon's RAW conversion software left a lot to be desired in the past. Canon has responded to the requests and complaints of photographers to develop a far superior RAW program, Digital Photo Professional (DPP). This optional software does not come with the EOS 20D, but is available from Canon and speeds processing quite noticeably, beating the old File Viewer Utility by a factor of five.

A key new feature is the ability of the program to save adjustments to a file that can then be reloaded and applied again to the original or to other RAW files. The program includes a whole range of valuable controls, including tone curves, exposure compensation, white balance, dynamic range, brightness, contrast, color saturation, ICC Profile embedding, and more. There is also a comparison mode that allows original and edited images to be compared side by side or in a split image.

DPP even has some batch processing features. It can allow continuous work on images while other files are rendered and saved in the background. Once images have been adjusted in DPP, they can be immediately transferred to Photoshop. There is no question that DPP will really help streamline the workflow of any photographer who needs to work with RAW.

Image Size and Quality

The EOS 20D offers a total of 13 choices for image-recording quality, consisting of combinations of different file formats, resolutions, and compression rates. But let's be straight about this, most photographers will shoot the maximum image size using the RAW or the highest-quality JPEG setting. There is little point in shooting smaller image sizes except for specialized purposes. After all, the camera's high resolution is what you paid for!

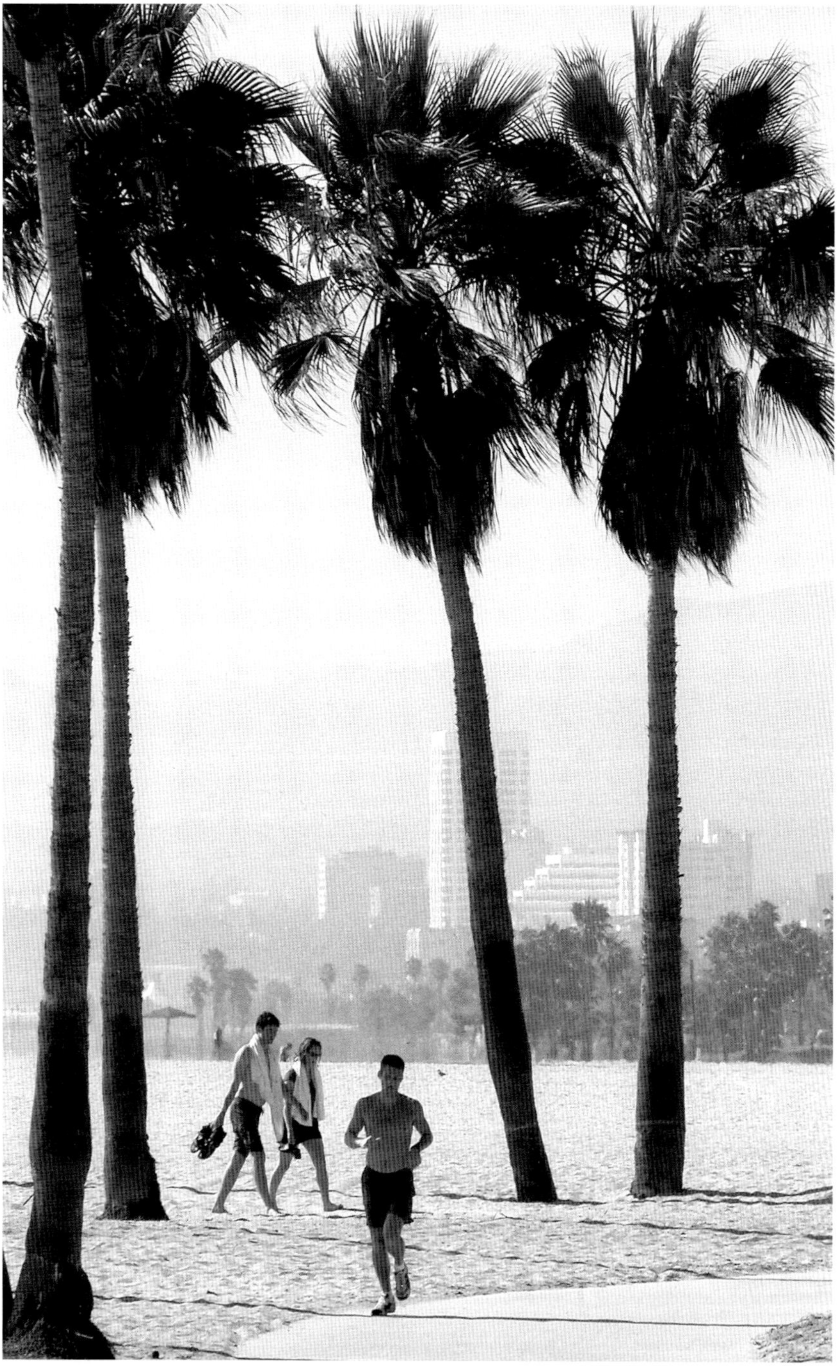

All settings for recording quality are selected in the Shooting menu under *Quality*. Press the SET button and the JPEG settings appear in the left-hand column, showing a symbol and a letter. The letter stands for the resolution size of the image file. The most important settings are L (the largest image size for JPEG, 8.2 megapixels) and RAW. RAW is always 8.2 megapixels.

The symbol depicts the level of compression. The shape with the smooth curve represents the least amount of compression (Fine = better quality), and when combined with L, makes a very high quality image. The symbol with a stair shape illustrates higher compression (Normal = lesser quality), giving a good quality JPEG image, but not as good as the Fine setting.

The 20D can record both RAW and JPEG simultaneously. Six different RAW+JPEG choices represent both Fine and Normal compression levels for each separate resolution of JPEG (L, M, S), and can be seen in the right-hand column of the menu screen. They can be useful for photographers who want added flexibility. These settings record images using the same identification numbers, but with different formats designated by their extensions, .jpg for JPEG and .cr2 for RAW. You can then use the JPEG file, for example, for direct printing, quick usage, and to take advantage of the DIGIC II processor. And you still have the RAW file for use when you need its added processing power.

RAW+ L is a key choice because you gain the best quality with the whole 8.2 megapixels in both formats. RAW+ S is useful for photographers who need to display a quick JPEG file for reference or to post on the web. This gives the full RAW file, plus a 2-megapixel JPEG file. These are the most commonly used RAW+JPEG files. The other combinations offer different options for resolution plus compression, but are usually useful only in specialized situations.

Even at a large setting for image size with low compression, you will be able to store far more image files on your CF card using JPEG rather than RAW format.

The RAW file will first appear in your RAW conversion software with the same details of processing as the JPEG file (including white balance, color matrix, and exposure), all of which can be easily changed in the RAW software. Though RAW is adaptable, it is not magic—you are still limited by the original exposure as well as the tonal and color capabilities of the sensor. Simply because RAW gives you more options to control the look of your images, it is not an excuse to become sloppy in your shooting. If you do not capture the best possible file, your results will be less than the camera is capable of producing.

Each choice does influence how many photos can fit on a memory card. Most photographers will be shooting with large memory cards because they will want the space required by high-quality files on this camera. It is impossible to give exact numbers of how many JPEG images will fit on a card because this compression technology is variable. You can change the compression as needed (resulting in varied file sizes), but remember, JPEG compresses each file differently depending on what is in the photo and how it can be compressed. For example, a photo with a lot of detail will not compress as much as an image with a large area of solid color.

That said, you may use the chart on page 75 to give you an idea of how large these files are and how many images might fit on a memory card of 1 gigabyte (GB)—the figures are based on actual numbers produced by the camera using such a card (JPEG values are always approximate). Also, the camera does use some space on the card for its own purposes, so you do not have access to the entire capacity of 1 GB for image files.

You can immediately see one advantage that JPEG gives over RAW in how a memory card is used. The highest-quality JPEG file at the full 8.2 megapixels allows you to store nearly 3.3 times the number of photos compared to what you could when shooting RAW.

File Sizes and Card Capacity

Image Size	File Size	Approximate Shots on 1 GB card
L	3.6 MB	240
L	1.8 MB	480
M	2.2 MB	420
M	1.1 MB	830
S	1.2 MB	730
S	0.6 MB	1440
RAW	8.7 MB	105
RAW + L	12.3 MB	72
RAW + S	9.3 MB	100

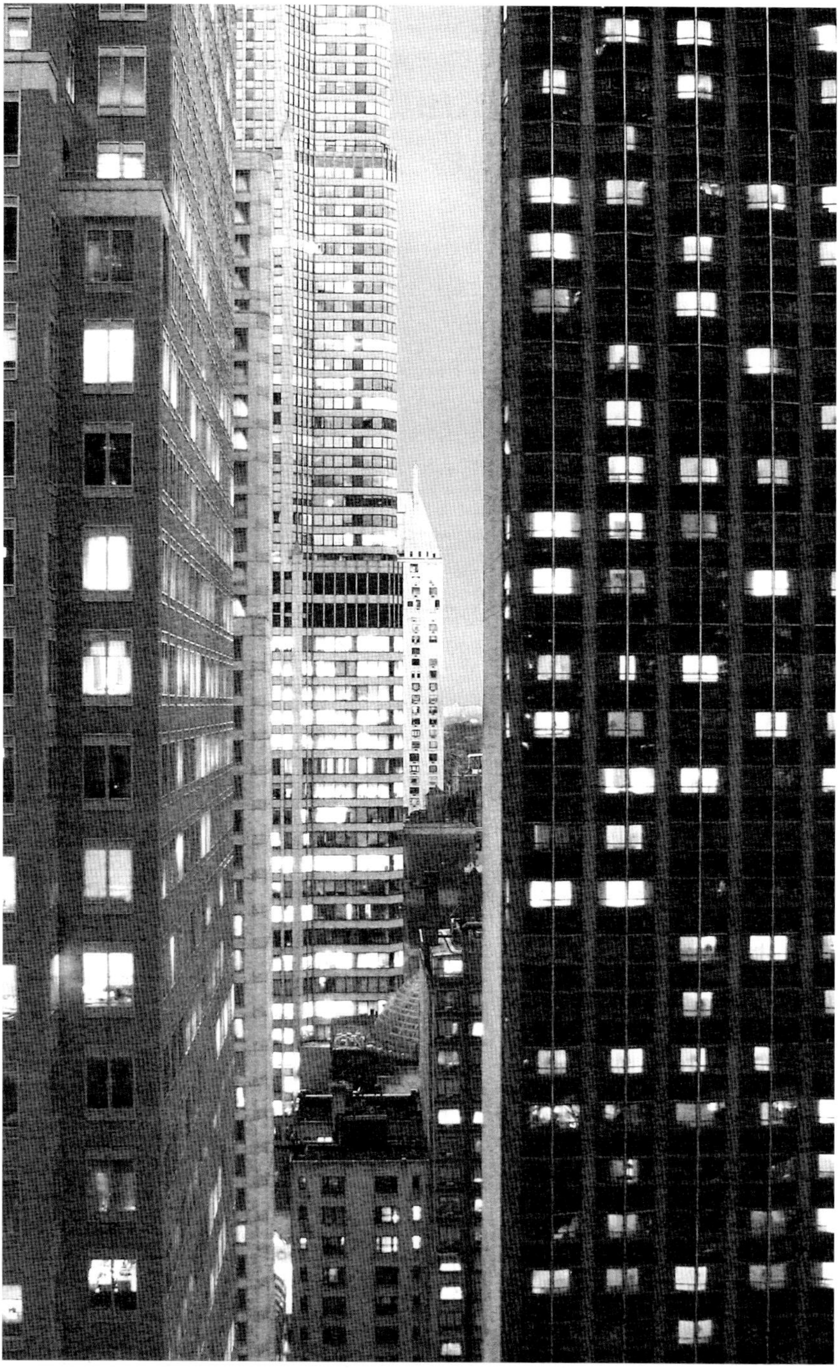

Camera Menus and the LCD Monitor

Using the Menus

Menus in digital cameras are a necessary evil—there are simply a great number of settings that need to be controlled. Still, in some cameras, menus are not always easy to use. Canon has put a great deal of thought into the design of the EOS 20D's menus so that they can be used efficiently. In addition, they can be set in 12 different languages.

All menu controls, or items, are grouped into three categories, based on their use. These categories, intuitively named in order of appearance within the menu system, are Shooting, Playback, and Set-up. You gain access to the 20D's menu selections whenever you push the MENU button, which is located on the back of the camera to the left of the LCD Monitor. At this point, the Shooting menu will appear. Move from category to category in one of two ways: push the JUMP button (also on back of camera to left of LCD Monitor) to enter the next one in order, or scroll down the items within any category to the bottom and automatically roll over to the next.

These category menus are designated by their icon at the top of the menu screen on the LCD Monitor. You actually see two icons; one at the top left of the screen for the category presently in use, and the next category's icon at the top right. Once in a menu category, rotate the Quick Control Dial to select desired items and sub items, and press the SET button to confirm, or lock-in, these item choices.

The camera's Auto Rotate function eliminates the need to turn the camera to view portrait-format images in the LCD Monitor. However, the image appears substantially smaller and more difficult to see.

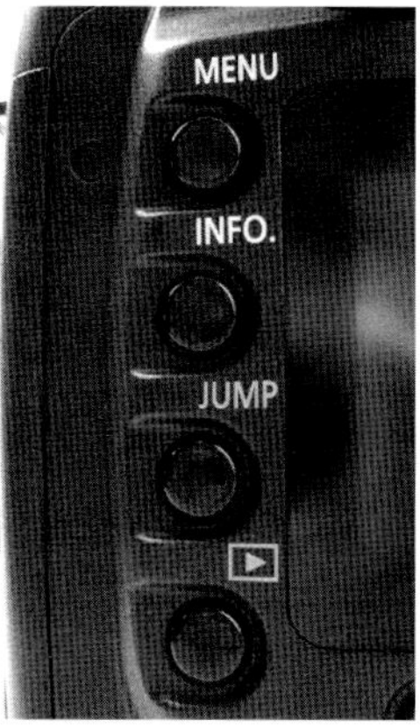

The MENU button, found to the left of the LCD Monitor, gives you the ability to select from a number of options and sub options for Shooting, Playback, and Set-up.

Shooting Menu

For items that obviously affect actual photography, this red-coded menu includes ten choices:
Quality (set image size and resolution, plus RAW)
Red-eye On/Off (set red-eye reduction)
Beep (signal for controls on or off)
Shoot w/o card (this allows you to test the camera when no memory card is in it)
AEB (auto exposure bracketing)
WB SHIFT/BKT (for bracketing and shifting white balance)
Custom WB (manually set white balance)
Color temp. (manually set color temperature)
Color space (sRGB or Adobe RGB)
Parameters (set up different profiles for processing images in-camera)

Playback Menu

Offers five choices used when viewing images on the LCD Monitor. This blue-coded menu includes:
Protect images (can't erase)
Rotate (rotate image so vertical will display vertically)
Print Order (specifies images to be printed DPOF)
Auto Play (automatic "slide show" on LCD Monitor changes image every 3 seconds)
Review time (how long image stays on LCD Monitor after shot)

Set-Up Menu

This menu is coded yellow.These are selections to make before shooting.

Auto power off (six time options or off)
Auto rotate (on/off)
LCD brightness (five levels)
Date/Time
File numbering options (two options)
Language (12 options)
Video system (NTSC or PAL)
Communication (for communicating with a printer)
Format (very important, used to initialize and erase the card)
Custom Functions (C.Fn)
Clear settings (make settings go back to default)
Sensor clean
Firmware Ver. (used when updating camera)

Understanding the menu system is necessary in order to gain full benefit from using the LCD Monitor and the Custom Functions.

The LCD Monitor

The LCD monitor is one of the most useful tools available when shooting digital, giving immediate access to your images. You can set your camera so that the image appears for review on the LCD monitor directly after shooting the picture. It's better than a Polaroid print!

The 20D's 1.8-inch color LCD Monitor is much brighter than the monitors of just a couple years ago, but it still takes a little practice to see it well in bright light. You can adjust its brightness in the Set-up Menu (select *LCD Brightness* and use the Quick Control Dial and SET button to adjust the brightness level and confirm), but this often makes the image harder to evaluate. The easiest thing to do is shade the monitor in bright light by using your hand, a hat, or your body to block the sun.

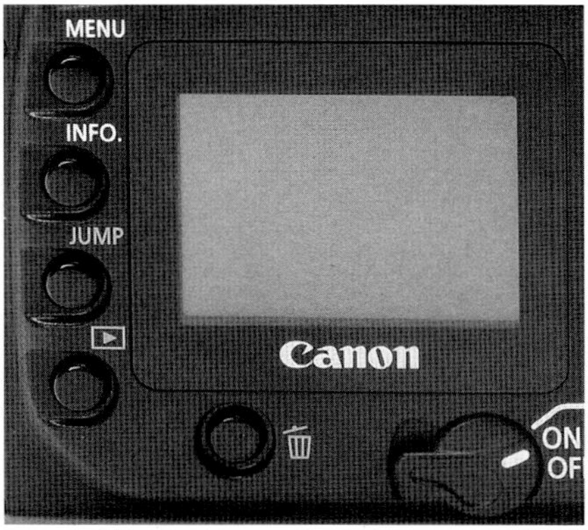

The bottom button in a column to the left of the LCD Monitor controls the image review and playback functions.

When photographers compare a point-and-shoot digital camera with a larger digital SLR, they often notice that the smaller camera's LCD monitor can be turned on while shooting. Digital point-and-shoot cameras have so-called "live" LCD monitors. However, like other digital SLRs, the 20D uses a mirror inside the camera (that blocks the path of light from subject to sensor) to direct the image from the lens to the viewfinder. During exposure, the mirror flips up exposing the sensor to light from the image. In order to "feed" a live LCD monitor, a camera's sensor must be able to see what is coming from the lens at all times.

LCD Image Review

The 20D's LCD Monitor, therefore, is used strictly for review and editing. You can choose to instantly review the image you have just shot, and you can also look at all of the images you have stored on your CF card. Most photographers like the instant feedback of reviewing their images because it gives a confirmation that the picture is okay.

You need to set the length of time needed to review the images you have just captured. It is frustrating to be examining a picture and have it turn off before you are done. You can set the duration from among a several choices that include *2 sec, 4 sec, 8 sec,* or *Hold,* all controlled by the *Review time* selection in the Playback menu ▶ (color code Blue). You also use this menu item to activate the *Off* option, which saves power by turning off the LCD Monitor, but does not allow you to review the images.

A setting of *2 sec* is a bit short—I prefer *8 sec*. You can always turn the review off sooner by pressing the Shutter button. The *Hold* setting is good if you like to study your photos, because the image for review remains on the LCD Monitor until you press the Shutter button. But be careful, it is easy to forget to turn off the monitor when using this selection, in which case your batteries will wear down.

Note: There is a trick not detailed in the camera manual that lets you "hold" the image even when the duration is not set to *Hold*. As the image appears for review, press the trash icon 🗑 (for erasing) located below the left corner of the LCD Monitor on the back of the camera. This will leave the image on as long as you want. Ignore the *OK* and *Cancel* commands. Press the Shutter button to turn the review image off.

Playback

Reviewing images on the LCD Monitor is an important benefit of digital cameras. To see not only your most immediate shot, but also any (or all) of the photos you have stored on the CF card, press the Playback button ▶ on the back of the camera to the left of the LCD Monitor. The last image you captured will show on the LCD Monitor. You then move from photo to photo by rotating the Quick Control Dial, either counterclockwise to view images in a sequence from most recent to first captured, or clockwise to view from first shot to most recent.

Note: Camera buttons with blue-colored labels or icons refer to playback functions.

The LCD Monitor not only displays images for review, but can also give you additional data about camera settings and exposure for each of your pictures.

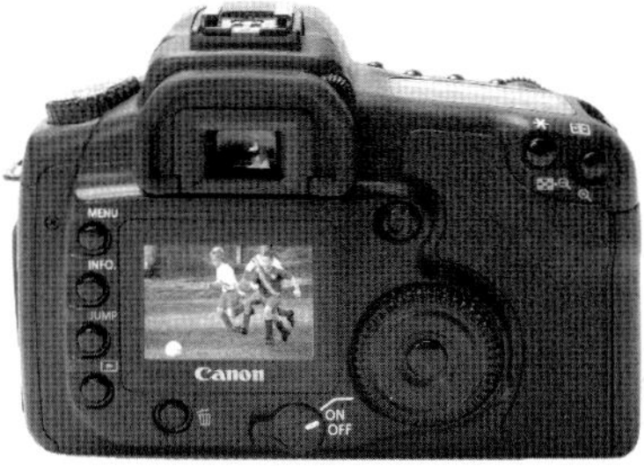

With the 20D, you can display the review or playback image in three different formats by progressively pushing the INFO button, also found on the back of the camera to the left of the LCD Monitor:

1. ***Display with basic information***—The image for review covers the entire LCD screen and includes superimposed data for folder number, image number, quantity of shots on the CF card, shutter speed, and aperture.

2. ***Display with full shooting information***—A thumbnail of the image is shown with a histogram and expanded data about how the image was shot (such as white balance, ISO speed, image recording quality, exposure, and more); this can be very useful for checking what settings are working for you. The thumbnail also includes a Highlight alert function that blinks where areas are overexposed.

3. ***Display with no information***—The image again covers the whole LCD Monitor, but only the image appears, no additional data about the picture is shown.

Pressing the Shutter button halfway will stop playback by turning the LCD Monitor off, making the 20D ready to shoot again. You can also stop the playback and turn the LCD Monitor off by pressing the Playback button.

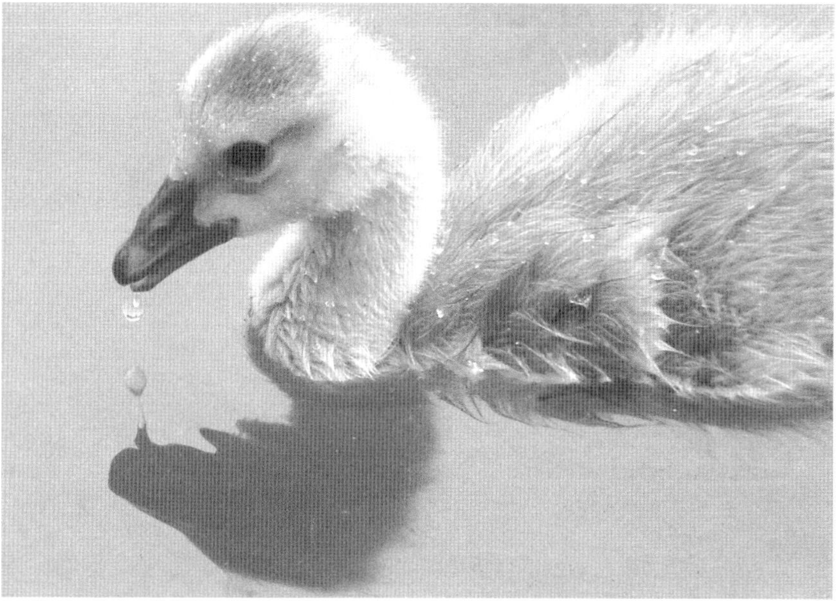

You can decide which shots to keep for downloading by reviewing your images on the LCD Monitor. Protect the ones you want to look at again, and delete those from your CF card that don't meet your standards. © Eric Dougherty

Automatic Image Rotation

Included in the 20D is an option to automatically rotate vertical images during review or playback so they appear up-and-down rather than sideways in the LCD Monitor when the camera is held in a horizontal position. To select this command, called *Auto rotate*, go to the Set-up menu and use the Quick Control Dial and SET button. Then choose *On*, again using the Quick Control Dial and SET button.

However, I must admit that I cannot recommend this feature. Sure, the image is upright and you don't have to rotate the camera to view it. The problem is the size of the image. To get that vertical image to fit in the horizontal frame of the LCD Monitor, the picture has to be reduced considerably and becomes harder to see. I like keeping *Auto rotate* off so the largest image shows up in the Monitor, even if I do have to rotate the camera to see it properly.

Magnifying the Image

You can make the image larger on the LCD Monitor by factors of 1.5x to 10x. This feature can be beneficial in helping to evaluate sharpness and exposure details. Press the Enlarge button ⊕ (located on back of camera in top right corner—marked by a blue magnifier with plus sign) repeatedly to progressively magnify the image. Press the Reduce button ⊖ (marked by a blue magnifier with minus sign), located to immediate left of the Enlarge button, to shrink the magnification. You quickly return to full size by pushing the Playback button.

Use the Multi-controller to move the magnified image around within the LCD Monitor in order to look at different sections of the picture. The Quick Control Dial will move from one image to another at the same magnified view so you can compare sharpness at a particular detail, for example.

Image Protection

I consider this feature to be one of the most underused and underappreciated functions of a digital camera. At first, it seems like no big deal—why protect your images? You take care of the memory card and promptly download images to the safety of your computer.

But that's not what image protection is about. Its most important function is to allow you to go through your pictures one at a time on the LCD Monitor, choosing which ones to keep, or "protect," meaning all the rest can be discarded.

Protection is very easy to use—go to the Playback menu and select *Protect*. Press the SET button and one image will appear in the LCD Monitor with a key symbol and the word SET appearing at the top left of the photo. Next go through your photos one by one using the Quick Control Dial and push the SET button for every one that is a potential "keeper." An icon showing a little key will now show at the bottom of the image.

Once you have chosen the protected images, select *All* on the Erase screen (see below), and all the images on the card are erased except the protected ones. You have now done a quick edit, giving you fewer photos to deal with after downloading to the computer. There is often downtime when shooting, so use it to go through your photos to edit by "protecting" key shots.

Erasing Images

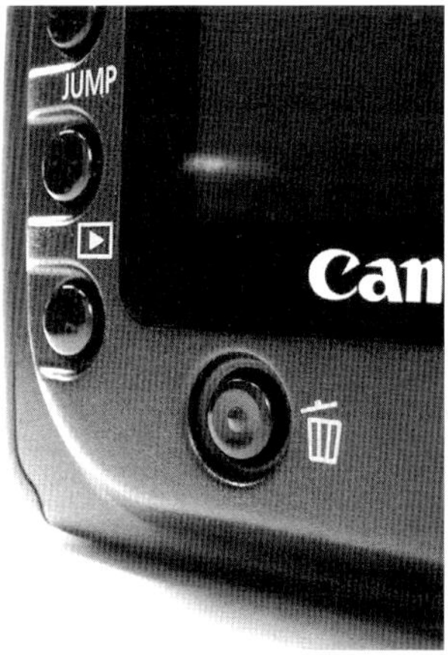

An icon of a trash barrel signifies the Erase button. It is located on the back of the camera, below the LCD Monitor.

The 20D's process for erasing photos from the memory card is the same as that used by most digital cameras. When an image is displayed on the LCD Monitor, push the Erase button 🗑 . Located below the LCD Monitor. A screen will appear with three options for erasing the image. Turn the Quick Control Dial to highlight the appropriate choice. The first option is *Cancel,* which will cancel this function. Next is *Erase,* which is the most commonly use function here and will erase the image being displayed. And last is *All,* to used if you want to delete all unprotected images on the CF card. You can erase images during playback or right after exposure when an image appears in review.

Note: Once an image is erased, it is gone for good. Make sure you no longer want an image before making the decision to erase it.

TV Playback

If you have a group of people who need to see your photos, and you have access to a television with standard RCA input connectors, you can display images on the TV from the memory card.

First, go to the Set-up menu and select the option for *Video system*. Then, if you are in the US or Canada, be sure to choose *NTSC*. (For many other parts of the world, you will need to select *PAL*). Make sure both the camera and television are turned off, then connect the camera to the TV using the cables supplied with the camera. Plug into the Video Out connector on the camera and Video In on the television. Turn the TV on, then the camera. Now press the Playback button and the image will appear on the TV (but not on the back of the camera). Some TV's will cut off edges of the image.

Custom Functions

Like most sophisticated cameras, either film or digital, the Canon EOS 20D can be customized to fit the unique needs and personality of a photographer. Of course, the selection of exposure modes, type of metering, focus choice, drive speed, and so forth do tailor the camera to a specific photographer's needs. However, the 20D allows for further customization and personalization to help the camera better fit your personality and style of photography. This is done through the Custom Functions menu. Some photographers never use these settings, while others use them all the time. The camera won't take better photos by changing these settings, but Custom Functions may make the camera easier for you to use.

The 20D has 18 different built-in Custom Functions (C.Fn), numbered 01-18. They are found in the Set-up menu under the selection for *Custom Functions (C.Fn)*. Use the Quick Control Dial to get to the C.Fn. option you want. (A helpful description of the control's function appears on the LCD Monitor as each is selected). Here is a brief summary and commentary on the various Custom Functions.

C.Fn-01 SET function when shooting
This setting assigns new options for using the SET button.

0. ***Default***—the SET button works normally, acting like an OK button for menus.
1. ***Sets recording quality***—allows you to press the SET button and go directly to recording quality. (This is useful if you want the ability to quickly change from RAW to JPEG). The settings appear in the LCD Panel.
2. ***Change parameters***—the SET button will take you directly to in-camera parameters (the parameters also show up on the LCD Panel).
3. ***Menu display***—SET acts like the MENU button (some people find this more convenient).
4. ***Replay***—the SET button acts like the Playback [▶] button.

C.Fn-02 Long exposure noise reduction
This is a simple on/off switch, which adds noise reduction for long exposures.

0. ***Off***—default
1. ***On***—long exposures will add noise, so this is a way of reducing it. However, this does add processing time, which will slow the camera (buSY will be displayed).

C.Fn-03 Flash sync speed in Av mode
This setting controls the camera-selected flash-sync speed in Av mode.

0. ***Default***—the camera varies the shutter speed to match the ambient light conditions.
1. ***1/250 fixed***—the camera always uses 1/250 sec. (This custom function doesn't seem to be particularly useful, since using Manual Exposure (M) mode at 1/250 then changing f/stop would give you the same feature without going through the menu).

C.Fn-04 Shutter button/AE Lock button

This controls the functions of the Shutter and AE Lock buttons

0. ***Default***—focus is locked when the Shutter button is depressed halfway; exposure is locked with the AE Lock button.
1. ***AE lock/AF***—autofocus is initiated with the AE Lock button. The Shutter button locks exposure when depressed halfway.
2. ***AF interrupt, no AE lock***—pressing the AE Lock button temporarily interrupts and locks focus in AI Servo AF mode. The exposure is set when the shutter releases. (This prevents focus from being thrown off if an object passes briefly in front of the camera.)
3. ***AF "pulse," no AE lock***—lets you start and stop AI Servo AF by pushing the AE Lock button. Exposure is set when the shutter releases.

C.Fn-05 AF-assist beam

This controls the AF-assist beam

0. ***Default***—the AF-assist beam is emitted whenever appropriate.
1. ***No AF assist***—this cancels the AF-assist beam, which can be useful in sensitive, low-light situations.
2. ***Disables built-in AF assist***—in low light, an accessory EX flash unit will fire its AF assist beam. The built-in flash's AF assist feature is always disabled.

C.Fn-06 Exposure level increments

This sets the size of incremental steps for shutter speeds, apertures, exposure compensation, and autoexposure bracketing (AEB).

0. ***Default***—the increment is 1/3 stop
1. ***1/2 stop***

C.Fn-07 Flash firing

This is used to disable either the built-in or accessory flash in sensitive situations.

0. ***Default***—flash fires whenever appropriate
1. ***Flash off***—flash will not fire under any circumstances.

C.Fn-08 ISO Expansion

This expands the ISO range of the camera to 3200.

0. ***Default***—ISO expansion is turned off.
1. ***On***—this expands the ISO settings to include 3200. "H" is the ISO setting for ISO 3200.

C.Fn-09 Bracket sequence/Auto cancel

This allows you to set the order of bracketed exposures and white balance or cancel bracketing.

0. ***Default order with auto cancel***—exposures will be made in this order: metered exposure, underexposure, and overexposure, with auto cancellation (meaning bracketing will be canceled if you change the lens or turn the camera off). White balance will be the set WB, then cooler (more blue) and warmer (more amber) or more magenta and green (which bias is dependent on how you set it up—see page 64 for WB bracketing).
1. ***Default order without auto cancel***—exposures will be made in the same order as above but there is no auto cancellation.
2. ***Optional order with auto cancel***—exposures will be made in this order: underexposure, metered exposure, and overexposure, with auto cancellation (meaning bracketing will be canceled if you change the lens or turn the camera off). White balance will be cooler (more blue), the set WB and warmer (more amber), or more magenta, the set WB and more green.
3. ***Optional order but no auto cancel***—this is the same as 2 but with no auto cancellation.

C.Fn-10 Superimposed display
This changes how the AF points appear in the viewfinder.

0. ***Default***—this illuminates or highlights the appropriate AF point when the camera locks focus (or points, depending on the AF mode).
1. ***Off***—turns off the illumination. Some photographers find the illuminated point distracting. The AF point will still light when you select it manually.

C.Fn-11 Menu button display position
This function changes how the menus are presented when you press the MENU button.

0. ***Default***—this shows the last menu item you looked at ("previous"), but will go to the top of the menu (Quality) if the switch is turned off, the battery is replaced, or the CF card is replaced.
1. ***Previous***—this does the same thing as above, but it always goes to the last menu item even if the camera is turned off.
2. ***Top***—this always displays the top menu screen (Quality).

C.Fn-12 Mirror lockup
This Custom Function turns mirror lockup on or off.

0. ***Default***—the mirror functions normally
1. ***Enabled***—the mirror will move up and lock in position with the first push of the Shutter button (press fully). With the second full pressing of the shutter button, the camera will then take the picture and the mirror will return to its original position. After 30 seconds, this setting automatically cancels.

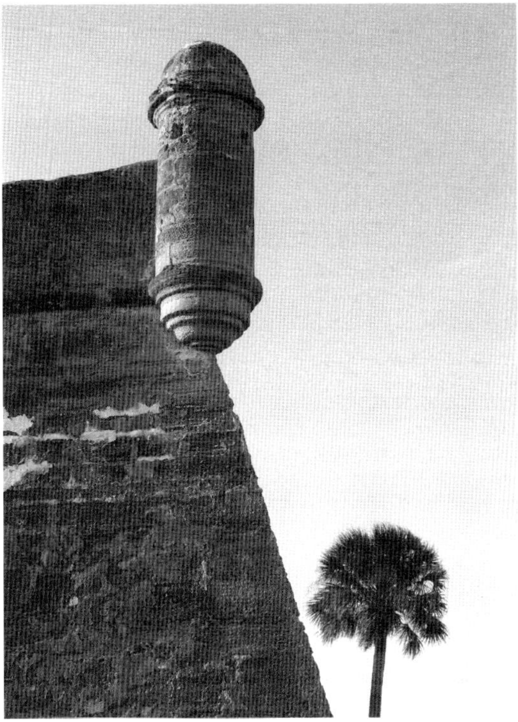

When manually selecting AF points, you can pick the precise subject area that you want the system to focus on.

C.Fn-13 AF point selection method

This control changes the how AF points are selected manually.

0. ***Default***—the AF point is selected using the AF point selection button [-:-] and the Multi-controller ✥.
1. ***Multi-controller direct***—this setting lets you select AF point using just the Multi-controller. The AF point selection button is used to set the camera back to auto AF point selection.
2. ***Quick Control direct***—this lets you use the Quick Control Dial ◯ for AF point selection. However, you must push the AF point selection button to use the Quick Control Dial for exposure compensation.

C.Fn-14 E-TTL II

This is a simple control that lets you choose a different way of metering electronic flash.

0. ***Default***—this uses fully automatic Evaluative metering for all conditions.
1. ***Average***—this setting averages the flash exposure readings over the entire area covered by the flash. Flash exposure compensation will not work with this setting.

C.Fn-15 Shutter curtain sync

This is a creative control that determines how motion blurs are rendered in flash photography.

0. ***Default, 1st curtain sync***—(also called front-curtain sync), this is the standard flash sync for most cameras, including the 20D. The flash goes off at the beginning of the exposure, as soon as the shutter curtains fully open to expose the whole sensor. At slow shutter speeds, the flash will create a sharp image and motion blur is registered after the flash. With moving subjects, this results in a blur or light trail that appears to be in front of the sharp flash-exposed subject (because the movement forward is after the flash). Such a blur is not natural looking.
1. ***2nd curtain sync***—(also called rear-curtain sync), the flash fires at the end of the exposure, just before the second shutter curtain closes. At slow shutter speeds, this results in an ambient light motion blur that looks natural because it trails behind a moving, sharp flash-exposed subject.

C.Fn-16 Safety shift in Av or Tv

You can allow the camera to smartly shift exposure when shooting in Av or Tv modes when the brightness of the scene exceeds the camera's capabilities at the chosen aperture or shutter speed.

0. ***Default, Disable***—this locks in the chosen f/stop for Av, or the shutter speed for Tv, regardless of conditions.
1. ***Enable***—this choice lets the camera shift f/stop or shutter speed to get a good exposure automatically.

C.Fn-17 Lens AF stop button function

This is a specialized function that only works with Canon's IS (Image Stabilized) lenses. If you don't have an IS lens, this custom function has no use.

0. ***Default, AF stop***—this is simply standard autofocus, but you can stop autofocus by pushing the AF stop button.
1. ***AF start***—autofocus operates only when the AF Stop button on the lens is pressed. AF operation with the camera itself will be disabled while the button is pressed.
2. ***AE lock while metering***—the AF Stop button locks exposure if it is pressed while metering is still active. This selection is great if you want to meter and focus a scene separately.
3. ***AF point M to auto***—holding down the AF Stop button will switch the camera from manual AF point selection to automatic AF point selection.
4. ***One shot to AI servo***—this choice enables the AF Stop button to switch the camera from One-Shot AF mode to AI Servo AF mode as long as the button is held down.
5. ***IS start***—with the lens' IS switch is turned on, the Image Stabilizer only operates when you press the AF Stop button.

C.Fn-18 Add original decision data

This very specialized setting is used by police and other law organizations.

0. ***Default***—Off.
1. ***On***—this turns the feature on so that data for verifying that images are original is added to the image file. To read this data, you need to use the optional Data Verification Kit DVK-E2.

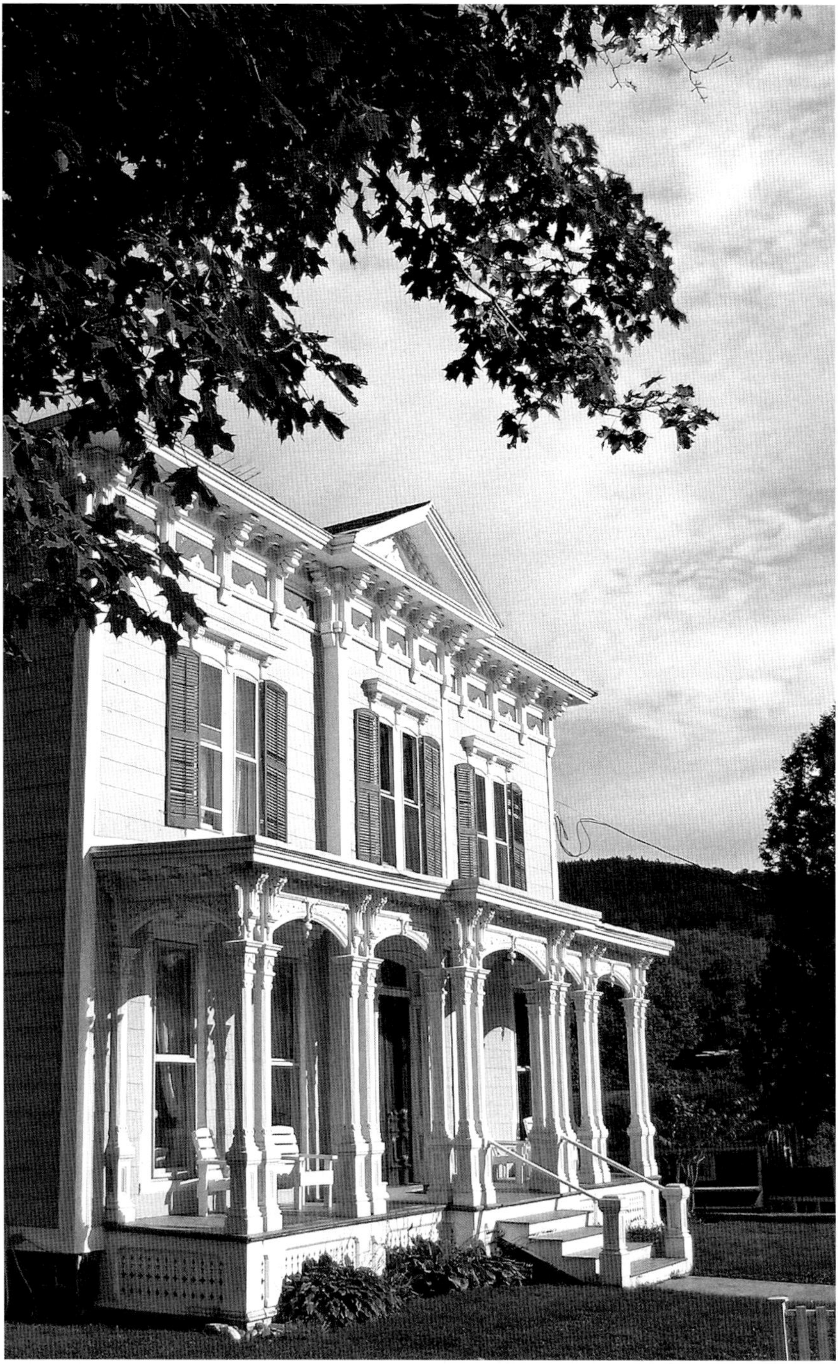

Camera Operation Modes

The 20D is a highly sophisticated and, in many ways, amazing digital camera. The innovation, thought, and technology that have been placed in this camera become evident as soon as you begin to operate its various systems and utilize its many functions. From finding focus on moving subjects to shooting multiple frames per second to capturing great exposures in low light, the 20D offers a number of options to help you take extraordinary photographs.

Focus

The 20D has an all-new, 9-point AF system using a special CMOS sensor dedicated to autofocus. It provides, for the first time in a camera at this price, full cross-type performance (a high-level way for an AF sensor to work) with maximum apertures as small as f/5.6 (again, unusual for a camera in this class). It also achieves autofocus three times faster than the EOS 10D when using lenses of f/2.8 or faster. The number of pixels on the central AF sensor is doubled compared to the 10D, which results in more consistent focus. The other eight sensors are placed near a golden section point (that mirrors classical art theories about composition), which results in more accurate autofocus with a whole range of pleasing compositions.

This new CMOS AF-sensor is the foundation of an innovative system that is designed to minimize ghosting, which can limit focusing performance. Unwanted light is blocked by a narrower field-of-view and low-reflectance materials in the sensor area. In addition, the AF optics and housing have a low expansion coefficient and low moisture absorption coefficient to keep autofocus consistent in all conditions.

The advanced technology and highly developed functions of the 20D give you the ability to capture great pictures every time you pick up your camera.

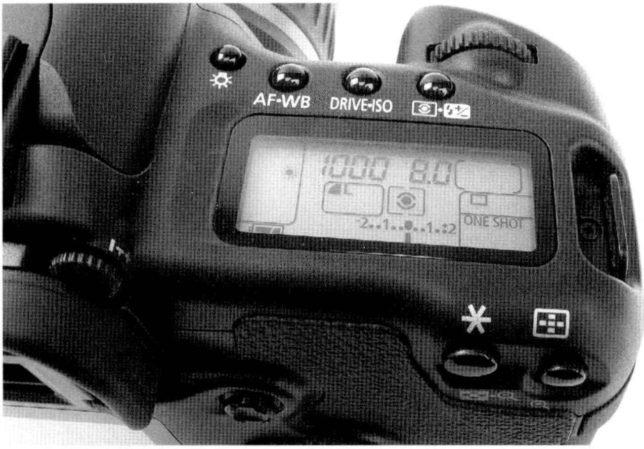

Select the AF mode you want by pressing the AF•WB button on top of the camera and scroll through the choices with the Main Dial until the desired mode appears in the LCD Panel.

The AF points work with an EV (exposure value) range of 0.5–18 (at ISO 100), one stop brighter than the 10D, and are superimposed in the viewfinder. They can be used automatically (the camera selects them as needed), or you can choose one manually. AF modes are selected by the photographer and include One-Shot AF, AI Servo AF, and AI Focus AF. Manual focusing is also an option.

The 20D smartly handles various functions of autofocus through the use of a high-performance, 32-bit microprocessor along with improvements in AF system design. The camera's ability to autofocus while tracking a moving subject is quite good. According to Canon for example, in AI Servo AF (continuous focus) with an EF 300mm f/2.8 USM lens, the 20D can focus-track a subject moving toward the camera at a speed of 186 mph up to about 66 feet (20 meters) away. It has the ability to very quickly employ statistical prediction while using multiple focusing operations to follow even an erratically moving subject. Yet, if the subject is not moving, the AI Servo AF focus control is notably stable—it will not allow the lens to change focus at all until the subject moves again.

When light levels are low, the camera activates AF assist with the built-in flash (external dedicated flashes also will do this). It produces a series of quick flashes to help autofocus. The range is to approximately 13 feet (4 meters) in the center of the frame and 11.5 feet (3.5 meters) at the other AF points. The 580EX Speedlite includes a more powerful AF-assist beam effective to 33 feet.

AF Modes

The camera has three AF modes in addition to manual focus: One-Shot AF (AF stops and locks when focus is achieved, one-shot at a time), AI Servo AF (this tracks subject movement and focuses continuously until the exposure is made), and AI Focus AF (the camera switches automatically between One Shot and Servo as it detects movement at the subject's position). In the Basic Zone, the AF mode is set automatically. In the Creative Zone, you can choose among all three; they are accessed by pressing the AF•WB button located on top of the camera in front of the LCD Panel. Use the Main Dial (on top of the camera behind the Shutter button) to scroll to the mode you want to use. Each is used for different purposes.

One-Shot AF: This AF mode finds and locks focus when you press the Shutter button halfway (exposure is also set). This is perfect for stationary subjects. It allows you to find focus and hold it at the important part of a subject. If the camera doesn't hit the right spot, it is a simple and quick matter to slightly change the framing and repress the Shutter button halfway to lock focus. Once you have found focus and locked, you can then move the camera to set the proper composition. The focus confirmation light will glow steadily in the viewfinder when you have locked focus. It will blink when the camera can't achieve focus. Since this camera focuses very quickly, a blinking light is a quick reminder that you need to change something (you may need to focus manually).

AI Focus AF: This mode allows the camera to choose between One-Shot and AI Servo. It can be used as the standard setting for the camera because it switches automatically from One-Shot to AI Servo if your subject should start to move. Note, however, that if the subject is still (like a landscape), this mode might detect other movement (such as a blowing tree), so it may not lock on the non-moving subject.

AI Servo AF: Great for action photography where subjects are in motion, AI Servo becomes active when you press the Shutter button down halfway, but it does not lock focus. It continually looks for the best focus as you move the camera or the subject travels through the frame. It is really designed for moving subjects, as both the focus and exposure are set only at the moment of exposure. This can be a problem to use for motionless subjects because the focus will continually change, especially if you are handholding the camera. However, if you are using AI Servo AF on a moving subject, it is a good idea to start the camera focusing (depressing the shutter halfway) before you actually need to take the shot so that the system can find the subject.

Selecting an AF Point: You can have the camera select the AF point automatically, or you can use the newly introduced Multi-controller to manually select a desired point. Manual AF point selection is useful when you have a specific composition in mind and the camera won't focus consistently where you want. To manually select an AF point, simply push the AF Point selection/Enlarge button and move the Multi-controller in any direction to select a focus point. Points light up as they are selected. If you push the controller to an already lit point, the camera automatically selects them all. Pressing in the center of the Multi-controller will automatically select the center point. It is an intuitive control that is simple to use. You can also go back to auto AF point selection quickly by pressing the Multi-controller twice in any direction.

You will be able to sharply capture moving subjects by using AI Servo AF mode.

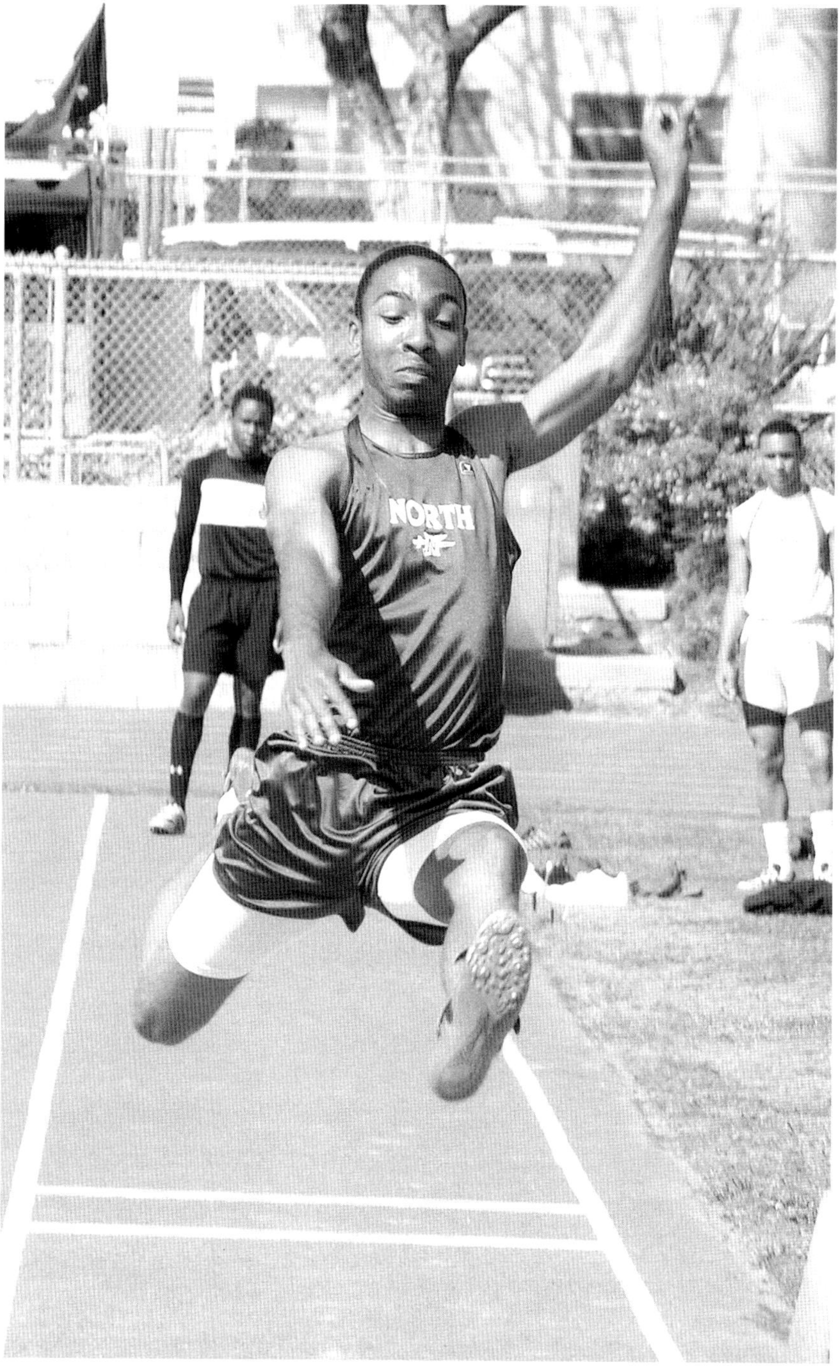
NORTH

You can also use the Main Dial to move through all the AF points, but this is much slower because you have to circulate through each point, one at a time.

AF Limitations: AF sensitivity is high with this camera. You will discover that the 20D can autofocus in conditions that are quite challenging for other cameras. Still, as the maximum aperture of lenses decreases, or tele-extenders are used, the camera's AF capabilities will change. It works its best with f/2.8 and wider lenses. It is important to realize that this is normal and not a problem with the camera.

It is possible for AF to fail in certain situations, therefore requiring you to focus manually. This would be most common where the scene is low-contrast or has a continuous tone (such as sky), in conditions of extremely low light, with subjects that are strongly backlit or have glare behind them, and with compositions that contain repetitive patterns. A quick and easy way of dealing with these situations is to move the camera to focus on something at the same distance as the rest of the photo, lock focus on it, then move the framing back to the original composition.

Drive Modes and the Self-Timer

The 20D offers two shooting speeds—Single shooting mode (one image at a time) or Continuous shooting mode (up to 5 frames per second). There is also an option for a 10-second self-timer. These are selected by pressing the DRIVE•ISO button then rotating the Main Dial. The chosen drive mode will appear in the LCD Panel as □ for Single shooting mode, as ⧉ for Continuous shooting mode, or as ⏲ for the Self-timer Operation.

The Self-timer is set for ten seconds and can be used in any situation where you need a delay between the time you press the Shutter button and when the camera actually fires. It can even be helpful when you are shooting slow shutter speeds on a tripod and can't (or don't want to) use a cable release. The ten-second delay allows camera vibrations to settle down before the shutter goes off (in the case of using the self-timer and mirror lock-up, the self-timer will use a two-second delay).

Exposure

No matter what technology is used to create a photo, it is always preferable to have the best possible exposure. Digital photography is no exception. A properly exposed digital file is one in which the right amount of light has reached the camera's sensor and produces an image that corresponds to the scene, or to the photographer's interpretation of the scene. This applies to color reproduction, as well as tonal values and subject contrast.

ISO

Before the advent of DX barcodes, the first step in getting the best exposure with film cameras was setting the ISO film speed. This provided the meter with information on the film's sensitivity to light, so that it could determine how much exposure would be required to record the image. Digital cameras adjust the sensitivity of the sensor circuits to settings that can be compared to film of the same ISO speed. (This change in sensitivity involves amplifying the electronic sensor data that creates the image.)

The 20D offers ISO sensitivity settings of 100-1600 but can also be set to "expand" to ISO 3200. This full ISO range is only available in the Creative Zone exposure modes (see page 111). In the Basic Zone modes (see page 108), ISO is set automatically from 100-400.

ISO is one control worth knowing so well that its use becomes intuitive. Its speed can be quickly set in the Creative Zone. Since sensitivity to light is easily adjustable using a digital SLR, and since the 20D offers clean images with minimal to no noise at any standard setting, ISO is a control to use freely so you can adapt rapidly to changing light conditions.

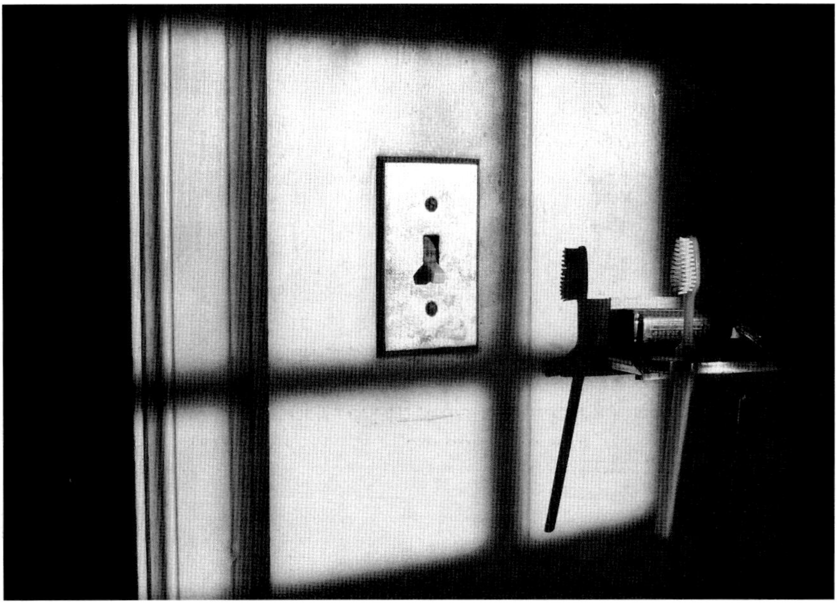

You can set the 20D to a higher ISO for indoor photogaphy without flash. The camera's exceptional noise control assures you will get great results even with moody black and white subjects such as this. ©Jeff Wignall

Low ISO settings give the least amount of noise and the best color. Traditionally, film would increase in grain and decrease in sharpness with increased ISO. This is not entirely true with the 20D because its image is extremely clean. Some increase in noise (the digital equivalent of grain) will be noticed as the higher ISO settings are used, but it is minimal until the highest settings of 800 and 1600 are chosen. Little change in sharpness will be seen. Even the settings of 800 and 1600 offer very good results. This opens your digital photography to new possibilities for using slow lenses (lenses with smaller maximum lens openings, which are usually physically smaller as well) and in shooting with natural light.

Setting the ISO: To set the ISO speed, press the DRIVE•ISO button located on the top of the camera in front of the LCD Panel. Then turn the Quick Control Dial until you see the desired displayed in the LCP Panel. The ISO settings occur in 1-stop increments (100, 200, 400, 800, 1600). Most of the time you will want to choose among several key ISO settings: 100 to capture detail in images of nature, landscape, and architecture; 400 when more speed is needed, such as handholding for portraits when shooting with a long lens; 800 and 1600 when you really need a lot of speed under low light conditions.

The camera also has a special ISO setting of 3200. Canon offers this as a specialized choice, available as Custom Function 08 (*ISO expansion*). The high speed of 3200 is distinctly noisier than lower settings, but if you are in a situation that requires such speed, the camera will give it to you. With *ISO expansion* selected to *on*, 3200 is added to the ISO choices. However, it does not appear as the number "3200." Instead, "H" appears in the LCD Panel.

Metering

In order to produce the proper exposure, the camera's metering system has to evaluate the light. However, even today there is no light meter that will produce a perfect exposure in every situation. Because different details of the subject reflect light in different amounts, the 20D's metering system has been designed with microprocessors and special sensors that give the system optimum flexibility and accuracy in determining exposure.

The camera offers three user-selectable methods of measuring light: Evaluative (linked to any desired AF point), Partial, and Center-Weighted. All three of these modes are set by pressing the Metering Mode Selection button on top of the camera in front of the LCD Panel and then rotating the Main dial . The symbol or icon for the type of metering in use appears on the LCD Panel.

Evaluative Metering: The 20D's Evaluative metering system divides the image area into 35 zones, 'intelligently' compares them, and then uses advanced algorithms to determine exposure. Basically, the system evaluates and compares all of the metering zones across the image, noting things like the subject's position in the viewfinder (based on focus points and contrast), brightness of the subject compared to the rest of the image, backlighting, and much more. These zones come from a grid of carefully designed metering areas that cover the frame, though fewer are at the edges.

As with all Canon EOS cameras, the 20D's Evaluative metering system is linked to autofocus. The camera actually notes which autofocus point is active and emphasizes the corresponding metering zones in its evaluation of the overall exposure. If the system detects a significant difference between the main point of focus and the different areas that surround this point, the camera automatically applies exposure compensation (it assumes the scene includes a backlit or spot-lit subject). However, if the area around the focus point is very bright or dark, the metering can be thrown off and the camera may underexpose or overexpose the image.

It is difficult to capture perfect exposures when shooting extremely dark or light subjects, subjects with unusual reflectance, or backlit subjects. Because the meter theoretically bases its analysis of light on an average gray scene, when subjects or the scene differ greatly from average gray, the meter will tend to overexpose or underexpose them. Luckily, you can check exposure information on the LCD Panel, or check the image itself on the LCD Monitor, and make adjustments as needed.

Note: With Evaluative Metering, after autofocus has been achieved, exposure values are locked as long as the Shutter button is partially depressed. However, meter readings cannot be locked in this manner if the lens is set for manual focus. You must use the AE Lock button in that case.

The main advantage of Evaluative metering over Partial and Center-weighted metering is that the exposure is biased toward the active AF point, rather than just concentrating on the center of the picture. Plus, Evaluative metering is the only metering mode that will automatically apply exposure compensation based on comparative analysis of the scene.

Partial Metering: Partial metering covers about 9% of the frame, utilizing the exposure zones at the center of the viewfinder. This allows the photographer to selectively meter portions of a scene and compare the readings in order to select the right overall exposure. This can be an extremely accurate way of metering, but it does require some experience to do well. When shooting with a telephoto lens, partial metering acts like spot metering.

Center-Weighted Metering: This method averages the reading taken across the entire scene, but in computing the "average exposure," the camera puts extra emphasis on the reading taken from center of the horizontal frame. Since most early traditional SLR cameras used this method exclusively, some photographers have used Center-weighted metering for such a long time that it is second nature and they prefer sticking with it. It can be very useful with scenes that change quickly around the subject.

One area in which to be careful with regard to exposure and this camera is the viewfinder eyepiece. This may sound odd, yet if you are shooting a long exposure on a tripod and do not have your eye to the eyepiece, there is a good possibility that your photo will be underexposed. The 20D's metering system is sensitive to light coming through an open eyepiece. To prevent this, Canon has included an Eyepiece cover on the camera strap that can be slipped over the viewfinder to block the opening in these conditions. You can quickly check the effect by watching the LCD Panel as you cover and uncover the eyepiece – you'll see how much the exposure can change.

Judging Exposure

The LCD Monitor allows you to get an idea of your photo's exposure—it's sort of like using a Polaroid, although it isn't as accurate. However, with a little practice, you can use this small image to evaluate your desired exposure, but realize that it only gives an indication of what you will actually see when the images are downloaded into your computer (because of the Monitor's calibration, size and resolution).

The EOS 20D includes two features that give you a good indication of whether or not each exposure is correct. These features, Highlight alert and the histogram, can be seen on the LCD Monitor once an image is displayed there. Push the INFO button repeatedly to cycle through a series of three displays: one shows the image along with exposure information, another is a small photo showing Highlight alert along with the histogram and exposure information, and the third shows the photo only (no info displayed).

Highlight Alert: The camera's Highlight alert is very straightforward: overexposed highlight areas will blink on the small photo with the histogram display. These areas have so much exposure that only white is recorded, no detail. It is helpful to immediately see what highlights are getting blown out, but some photographers find the blinking is a distraction. Blinking highlights are simply information, and not necessarily bad. Some scenes have less important areas that will get washed out if the most important parts of the scene are exposed correctly. However, if you discover that significant parts of your subject are blinking, the image is likely overexposed. You need to reduce exposure in some way.

The Histogram: The 20D's histogram, though small, is a very important tool for the digital photographer. It is the graph that appears on the LCD Monitor next to the image when selected with INFO during review or playback, indicating the image's brightness.

The horizontal axis of the histogram indicates the level of brightness—dark areas are at the left, bright areas are at the right. The vertical axis indicates the pixel quantity existing for the different levels of brightness. If the graph rises as a slope from the bottom left corner of the histogram, then descends towards the bottom right corner, all the tones of the scene are captured.

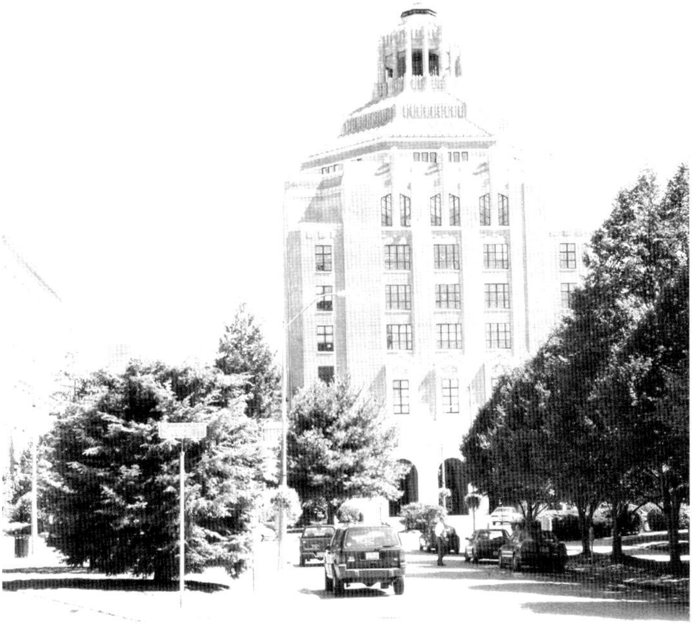

Pictures lose detail in the light areas of a scene when they are beyond the camera's dynamic range. The Highlight alert and histogram features tell you when a picture has been "blown out." ©K. Kopp

Consider the graph from left to right (dark to bright). If the graph itself starts too high on either end, i.e., so the "slope" looks like it is abruptly cut off at either side, then the exposure data is also cut off or "clipped" at the ends because the sensor is incapable of handling the areas darker or brighter than those points. An example would be a dark, shadowed subject on a bright, sunny day. In addition, the histogram may be weighted towards either the dark or bright side of the graph (wider, higher "hills" appear on one side or the other). This is okay if the subject is mostly dark or bright, but if it is not, detail may be lost. The dark sections of your photo may fade to black (with increased noise there), and brighter sections may appear completely washed out.

If highlights are important, be sure that the slope on the right reaches the bottom of the graph before it hits the right side. If darker areas are important, be sure the slope on the left reaches the bottom before it hits the left side. You don't actually have to remember which side is dark or light at first. If you notice an unbalanced graph, just give the scene a change of exposure and notice which way the histogram changes. This is a really good way to learn to read the histogram.

Some scenes are naturally dark or light. In these cases, most of the graph can be on the left or right, respectively. However, be careful of dark scenes that have all the data in the left half of the histogram. Such underexposure tends to overemphasize any sensor noise that might be present. You are better off increasing the exposure, even if the LCD image looks bright enough. You can always darken the image in the computer, which will not affect grain; yet lightening a very dark image usually will have an adverse effect and result in added noise.

If the scene is low in contrast and the histogram is a rather narrow hill in the middle of the graph, check the 20D's processing parameter settings. Boosting contrast will expand the histogram—you can create a custom setting with contrast change and tonal curve adjustments that will consistently address such a situation. This can mean better information being captured since it is spread out more evenly across the tones before bringing the image into your computer to use image-editing software. In addition, this type of histogram is a good condition for using RAW, since the stretching of data to better use the tonal range from black to white looks best in RAW.

Basic Zone Shooting Modes

The 20D offers twelve exposure, or shooting, modes divided into two groups: the Basic and the Creative Zones. In the Basic Zone, the primary benefit is that the camera can be matched quickly to conditions or to a subject. Fast and easy to manage, the modes in the Basic Zone permit the camera to predetermine a number of settings. Exposure, ISO, and white balance are set automatically in all Basic Zone modes, while the metering method is Evaluative. In some of these modes, all the controls are set by the camera and cannot be adjusted by the photographer.

All exposure modes, including the Basic Zone modes, are selected by using the Mode Dial on the top left of the camera. Simply rotate the dial to the icon you wish to use.

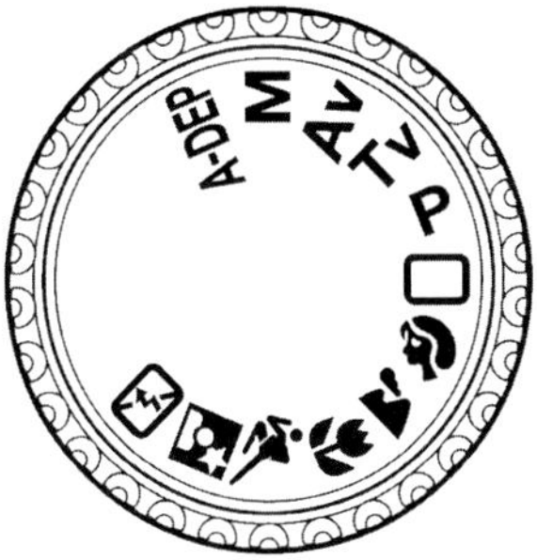

Point the Mode Dial at your desired icon to select one of twelve different exposure modes.

Full Auto: For completely automatic shooting, this mode essentially converts the 20D into a point-and-shoot camera (a very sophisticated point-and-shoot!). The camera chooses everything—you cannot adjust any controls. This mode is really designed for the beginning photographer who does not trust his or her decisions, or for situations when you hand the camera to someone to take a picture of you (that way they can't mess up settings).

Portrait: If you like to shoot portraits, this makes adjustment choices that favor people photography. The drive is set to Continuous so you can quickly shoot changing gestures and expressions, while the AF mode is set to One-Shot so you can lock focus with a slight pressing of the shutter release. The meter favors wider f/stops (those with smaller numbers) because this limits depth of field, offering backgrounds that are softer and therefore contrast with the sharper focus of the subject. A wider f/stop also results in faster shutter speeds, resulting in sharper handheld images.

Landscape: It is important to lock focus on one shot at a time, so Landscape mode uses One-Shot AF and the Single shooting drive mode. The meter favors small f-stops for more depth-of-field (often important for scenic shots), plus the camera chooses the more saturated Parameter 1 setting (all other Basic Zones use the default Parameter 2).

Close-Up: This zone also uses One-Shot AF and the Single shooting modes. It favors wider f/stops for faster shutter speeds giving better sharpness with a handheld camera, and for less depth of field in order to set a sharp subject off against a softer background and to employ .

Sports: Designed for action and fast shutter speeds to stop that action, Sports mode uses AI Servo AF and the Continuous drive mode, both of which allow continuous shooting as action evolves in front of you. In addition, the beep for AF confirmation will be softer than other modes.

Night Portrait: Very useful to help even advanced photographer balance flash with low light conditions (does not have to be night). This uses flash to illuminate the subject (which may or may not be a portrait), then uses an exposure to balance the background, bringing in its detail. The latter exposure, called the ambient light exposure, can have a very slow shutter speed, which may mean a blurry background (which can be very trendy looking or just unpleasant), so you may need a tripod.

Flash Off: Provides a quick and easy setting that prevents the flash from firing, which can be important in museums and other sensitive locations.

Creative Zone Modes

The Creative Zone modes offer complete control over camera adjustments and thus encourage a more creative approach to photography. The disadvantage is that there are many possible adjustments, which can be confusing at the worst, and time consuming at best. Again, all modes in the Creative Zone are engaged by turning the Mode Dial to the desired designation. Adjustments to the settings, which are displayed in the LCD Panel and viewfinder, are made by turning the Main Dial.

Program AE Mode (P): In Program AE (autoexposure), the camera chooses the shutter speed and aperture combination. This gives the photographer less direct control over the exposure because no matter how apt, the settings are chosen arbitrarily (by the camera, not you). However, you can "shift" the program by changing either the selected aperture or shutter speed, and the system will compensate to maintain the same exposure value. To shift the program, simply press the Shutter button halfway, then turn the Main Dial or Quick Control Dial until the desired shutter speed or aperture value (respectively) is displayed. This only works for one exposure at a time, making it useful for quick-and-easy shooting while retaining some control over camera settings.

Program AE mode selects shutter speed and aperture values "steplessly." This means that any shutter speed or aperture within the range of the camera and lens will be selected, not just those that are the standard full steps, such as 1/250 second or f/16. This has been common with most SLRs (both film and digital) for many years and allows for extremely precise exposure accuracy, thanks to the lens' electromagnetically controlled diaphragm and the camera's electronically timed shutter.

If the system determines there is risk of a bad exposure, the shutter speed and aperture values will blink in the viewfinder. When this occurs because there is too much light, a neutral-density (ND) or polarizing filter can be used to reduce the light coming into the lens. You can also decrease the ISO setting. If there is insufficient light, either increase the ISO speed or try using a larger aperture (smaller f/number).

Shutter-Priority AE Mode (Tv): Tv (which stands for "time value") signifies Shutter-Priority AE. Shutter-Priority means that you set the shutter speed and the camera sets the aperture. If you want a particular shutter speed for artistic reasons—perhaps a high speed to stop action or a slow speed for blur effect—this is the setting to use. In this mode, even if the light varies, the shutter speed will not. The camera will keep up with changing light by adjusting the aperture automatically. If the aperture indicated in the viewfinder or the LCD Panel is consistently lit (not blinking), evaluative metering has picked a useable aperture. If the maximum aperture (lowest number) blinks, it means the photo will be underexposed and you need to select a slower shutter speed by turning the Main Dial until the aperture indicator stops blinking. You can also remedy this by increasing the ISO speed. If the minimum aperture (highest number) is blinking, this indicates overexposure. In this case, you should set a faster shutter speed until the blinking stops, or choose a slower ISO speed.

The 20D offers a choice of speeds, from 1/8000 second up to 30 seconds in 1/3-stop increments, plus Bulb setting. For flash exposures, the camera will sync at 1/250 second or slower (which is important to know since slower shutter speeds can be used to pick up ambient or existing light in a dimly-lit scene). Let's examine these shutter speeds by designating them "fast," "moderate," and "slow." (These divisions are arbitrarily chosen, so speeds at either end of the divisions can really be designated into the groups on either side of them.)

Fast shutter speeds are 1/500–1/8000 second. It wasn't all that long ago that most film cameras could only reach 1/1000 second, so having this range of high speeds on a digital SLR is quite remarkable. The obvious reason to choose these speeds is to stop action. The more the action increases in pace, or the closer it crosses directly in front of you, the higher the speed you will need. As mentioned previously, the neat thing about a digital camera is that you can check your results immediately on the LCD monitor to see if the shutter speed has in fact frozen the action.

At these fast speeds, camera movement during exposure is rarely significant unless you try to handhold a super telephoto lens of 600mm (not recommended!). This means with proper handholding technique, you can shoot using most normal focal lengths (from wide-angle to telephoto up to about 300mm) with few problems from camera movement. Besides stopping action, another important use of the high shutter speeds is to allow you to use your lens at its wide openings (such as f/2.8 or f/4) for selective focus effects (shallow depth of field). In bright sun, for example, you might have an exposure of 1/200 second at f/16 with an ISO setting of 200. You can get to f/2.8 by increasing your speed by five whole steps of exposure, to approximately 1/4000 second.

Moderate shutter speeds (1/60–1/250 second) work for most subjects and allow a reasonable range of f/stops to be used. They are the real workhorse shutter speeds, as long as there's no fast action. You do have to be careful when handholding cameras at the lower end of this range, especially with telephoto lenses, or you may notice blur in your pictures due to movement of the camera during the exposure. Many photographers find that they cannot handhold a camera with moderate focal lengths (50-150mm) at shutter speeds less than 1/125 second without some degradation of the image due to camera movement. You can double-check your technique by taking a photograph of a scene while handholding the camera, and then comparing the same scene shot using a tripod.

Slow shutter speeds (1/60 second or slower) require something to stabilize the camera. Some photographers may discover they can handhold a camera and shoot relatively sharp images at the high end of this range, but most cannot get optimal sharpness from their lenses at these speeds without a tripod or other stabilizing mount. Slow shutter speeds are used mainly for low light conditions and to allow the use of smaller f/stops (higher f/stop numbers) under all conditions.

A fun use of very slow shutter speeds (1/8–1/2 second) is to photograph movement, such as a waterfall or runners, or to move the camera during exposure, such as panning it across a scene. The effects are quite unpredictable, but again, image review using the LCD Monitor helps. You can try different shutter speeds and see what they look like. This is helpful when trying to choose a slow speed appropriate for the subject because each speed will blur action differently.

You can set slow shutter speeds (up to 30 seconds) for special purposes such as capturing fireworks or moonlit landscapes. Canon has engineered the sensor and its accompanying circuits to minimize noise (a common problem of long exposures with digital cameras) and the 20D offers remarkable results with these exposures.

In contrast to long film exposures, long digital exposures are not susceptible to reciprocity. The reciprocity effect comes with film because as exposures lengthen beyond approximately 1 second (depending on the film), the sensitivity of the film declines, resulting in the need to increase exposure to compensate. A metered 30-second film exposure might actually require double or triple that time to achieve the effect that is desired. Digital cameras do not have this problem. A metered exposure of thirty seconds is all that is actually needed.

The setting for Bulb Exposure allows you to control long exposures (buLb follows 30 seconds when scrolling through shutter speeds). With this option, the shutter stays open as long as you keep the Shutter button depressed. Let go and the shutter closes. Two dedicated remote switches, the Canon RS-80N3 and TC-80N3, are very helpful for these long exposures, since they allow you to keep the shutter open without touching the camera (which can cause movement)—they attach to the camera with quick-lock plugs to the remote terminal on the left side. You can use the infrared LC-4 wireless remote switch for bulb exposures, as well.

The camera will show the elapsed time for your exposure as long as you keep the remote switch depressed. This can be quite helpful in knowing your exposure. The elapsed time is shown in seconds. At this point in digital camera technology, exposures beyond a few minutes start to have serious problems. Still, the 20D does allow longer exposures than most cameras of this type, and it is a good idea to use the noise reduction selection in the camera menu—this will apply added in-camera noise reduction.

Aperture-Priority AE Mode (Av): When you select Av (aperture value), you are in Aperture-Priority AE mode. In this autoexposure mode, you set the aperture (the f/stop or lens opening) and the camera selects the proper shutter speed for a proper exposure. This is probably the most popular automatic setting among professional photographers.

Controlling depth of field is one of the most common reasons for using Aperture-Priority mode. (Depth of field is the distance in front of and behind a specific plane of focus that is acceptably sharp.) While the f/stop, or aperture, affects the amount of light entering the camera, it also has a direct effect on depth of field. A small lens opening (higher f/number) such as f/11 or f/16 will increase the depth of field in the photograph, bringing objects in the distance into sharper focus (when the lens is focused appropriately). Higher f/numbers are great for landscape photography.

A wide lens opening with low f/numbers such as f/2.8 or f/4 will decrease the depth of field. These lower f/numbers work well for when you want to take a photo of a sharp subject that creates a contrast with a soft, out-of-focus background. If the shutter speed is blinking in the LCD Panel, it means good exposure is not possible at that aperture, so you either need to change the aperture or ISO setting.

You can see the effect of the aperture setting on the image by pushing the Depth-of-Field Preview button on the camera (located on the lower left of the front lens housing, below the Lens Release button). This stops the lens down to the taking aperture and reveals sharpness in the resulting darkened viewfinder (the lens otherwise remains wide-open until the next picture is taken). Using Depth-of-Field Preview takes some practice because of the viewfinder darkness. But changes in focus can be seen if you look hard enough. You can also just check focus in the LCD Monitor after the shot (magnify it as needed), since digital allows you to both review and/or delete your photos as you go.

A sports or wildlife photographer might choose Av mode in order to stop action rather than to capture depth of field. To accomplish this, he or she selects a wide lens opening—perhaps f/2.8 or f/4—to let in the maximum amount of light. In Av mode, the camera will then automatically select the fastest shutter speed possible for the conditions. With Tv mode, while you can set a fast shutter speed, the camera still may not be able to expose correctly if the light drops and the selected shutter speed requires an opening larger than the particular lens can provide (the aperture value will blink in the viewfinder in such a case). So typically photographers will select Tv only when they have to have a specific shutter speed. Otherwise they use Av for both depth of field and to gain the highest possible shutter speed for the circumstances.

Automatic Depth-of-Field AE (A-DEP): This is a unique exposure mode that Canon has used on a number of EOS SLR's (both film and digital) over the years. A-DEP simplifies the selection of an f/stop to ensure maximum depth of field for a subject. The camera actually checks focus, comparing all nine AF points to determine the closest and farthest points in the scene. The camera then picks an aperture to cover that distance and the appropriate shutter speed. You cannot control either yourself. It also sets the focus distance. If the camera cannot get an aperture to match the depth of field needed to cover the near and far points, the aperture will blink. You can check what the depth of field looks like by pushing in the Depth-of-Field Preview button. You have to use AF on the lens; MF will make the camera act like P was set. A-DEP also does not work with flash, and the camera will also act like P was set.

Manual Exposure Mode (M): Not an auto mode, the Manual Exposure option is important for photographers who are used to working in full manual (although I would suggest that everyone at least try the automatic settings at times to see what they can do—this camera is designed to give exceptional autoexposures), and also for anyone who faces certain tricky situations. In Manual Exposure, you set both the shutter speed (using the Main Dial) and aperture (set the Power switch ON to the angled line, then turn the Quick Control Dial). You can use the exposure metering systems of the camera—exposure is visible on the scale at the bottom of the Viewfinder information display. "Correct" exposure is at the mid-point, and you can see how much the exposure settings vary from that point by observing the scale. It shows up to two f/stops over or under the mid-point, which can allow you to quickly compensate for bright or dark subjects (especially when using Partial metering). If part of the scale blinks, the exposure is off the scale. Of course, you can also use a hand-held meter.

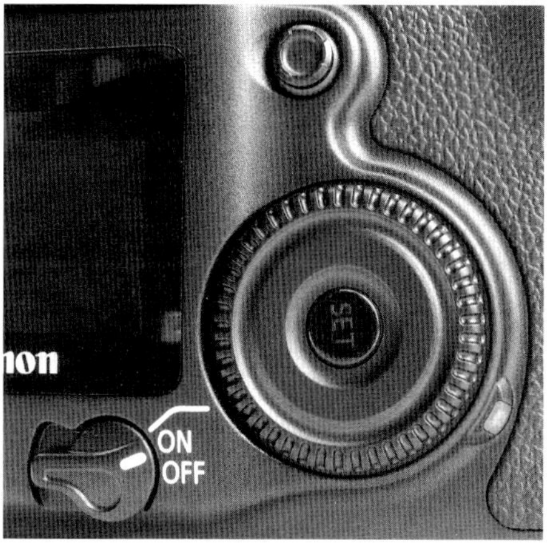

Point the Power switch to the angled line to control aperture settings in Manual Exposure mode.

The following examples of complex metering conditions might require you to use M mode: panoramic shooting (you need a consistent exposure across the multiple shots taken, and the only way to ensure that is with Manual); lighting conditions that change rapidly around a subject with consistent light (a theatrical stage, for example); close-up photography where the subject is in one light but slight movement of the camera dramatically changes the light behind it; and any conditions where you need a consistent exposure through varied lighting conditions.

* AE Lock

AE Lock is a very useful tool in the autoexposure modes. Under normal operation, the camera continually updates exposure either as you move the camera across the scene or as the subject moves. This can be a problem if the light across the area is inconsistent yet remains constant on the subject. You will want to lock the exposure on the subject. This tool is also helpful when a scene is mostly in one light, yet your subject is in another. In that circumstance, try to find a spot nearby that has the same light as your subject, point the camera at it and lock exposure, then move the camera back to the original composition.

AE Lock on the 20D is similar to that used for most EOS cameras. Its button is signified by an asterisk and is located on the back of the camera to the upper right.

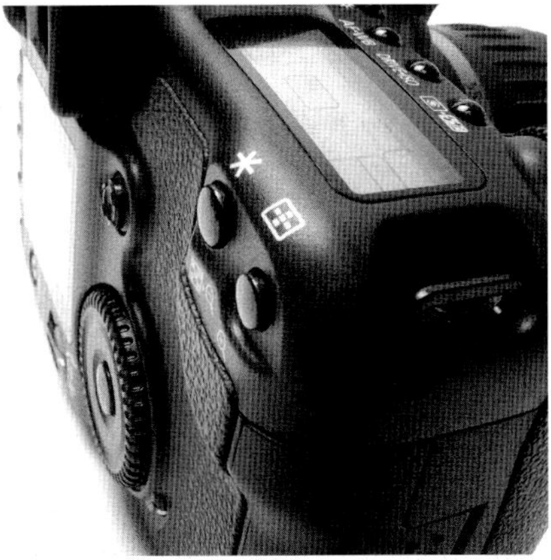

*The AE Lock button, indicated by * , allows you to take an exposure reading on a subject or specific area. You can then recompose the picture and the locked-in meter reading will not change.*

Aim the camera where needed for the proper exposure, then push this button. The exposure is "locked," or frozen, even if you move the camera. An asterisk will appear in the Viewfinder information display. The exposure scale on the right side gives important data—it compares the locked exposure in the center with the "present exposure" of the composition (the second dot). If you don't like what the lock gave for exposure, you can change it by pressing the AE Lock button again. You can also shift exposure by using the Main Dial or apply a degree of compensation with the Quick Control Dial.

Exposure Compensation

The existence of a feature for exposure compensation, along with the ability to review images in the LCD Monitor, means you can quickly get good exposures without using Manual Exposure mode. Exposure compensation cannot be used in M mode. However, it makes the P, Tv, Av and A-DEP modes much more versatile. Compensation is added (for brighter exposure) or subtracted (for darker exposure) in f/stop increments of 1/3 for up to +/- 2 stops.

It only works if the camera is active (i.e., you see both shutter speed and aperture in the Viewfinder information display) and works quite easily with the Quick Control Dial switched on (when the on switch is set to the angled line). Simply press the Shutter button halfway to turn on the metering system, then use your thumb to rotate the Quick Control Dial to change the compensation amount. You will see the exact exposure compensation on the scale at the bottom of the Viewfinder information display, as well as on the LCD Panel.

It is important to remember that once you set your Exposure Compensation control, it stays set even if you shut off the camera. Check your exposure setting as a regular habit (by looking at the bottom scale in the Viewfinder information display) when you turn on your camera to be sure the compensation is not inadvertently set for a scene that doesn't need it. With experience, you will find that you use exposure compensation routinely with certain subjects. Remember, the meter wants to increase exposure on dark subjects and decrease exposure on light subjects to make them closer to middle gray. For this reason exposure compensation may be necessary.

For example, say you are photographing a high school soccer game with the sun behind the players. The camera wants to underexpose in reaction to the bright sunlight, but the shaded sides of the player's bodies may be too dark, so you add exposure with the 20D's Exposure Compensation feature. Or maybe the game is in front of densely shaded bleachers. In this case the players would be overexposed because the camera wants to react to the darkness. Here, you subtract exposure. In both cases, the camera will consistently maintain the exposure you have selected until you readjust the exposure settings.

The LCD Monitor can come in handy when experimenting with exposure compensation. Take a test shot, then check the photo and its histogram. If it looks good, go with it. If the scene is too bright, subtract exposure; if it's too dark, add it. Again, remember that if you want to return to making exposures without using compensation, you must move the setting back to zero!

Autoexposure Bracketing (AEB)

The 20D also offers another way to apply exposure compensation—by using the Autoexposure Bracketing control (AEB). AEB tells the camera to make three consecutive exposures that are different: (1) a standard exposure (it will use any setting of the Exposure Compensation function as the standard); (2) one with less exposure; and (3) one with more (this can be changed with Custom Function 09). The difference between exposures can be set up to +/- 2 stops in stop increments of 1/3 (Custom Function 6 will allow you to change this to 1/2 increments). AEB is set through the Shooting menu . Scroll to *AEB* with the Quick Control Dial, press Set, then use the Quick Control Dial again to set the amount. Three dots will appear on a small exposure scale on this menu (they will also appear on the LCD Panel). These indicate the range of exposures. Press set to accept the change.

As you shoot, you will also see a marker appear on the exposure scale at the bottom of the Viewfinder information display. This marker indicates which exposure is being used with the AEB sequence. When in Single shooting mode, you have to press the Shutter button for each of the three shots. In Continuous shooting modes, the camera will take the three shots and stop. With the Self-timer, all three shots will be taken. While utilizing AEB, the 20D will change shutter speed in Tv mode and aperture in Av mode. If you use AEB, remember that the camera will continue to take three different exposures in a row until you reset the control to zero, turn the camera off, change lenses, or replace the CF card.

AEB can help ensure that you get the best possible image files for later adjustment using image-editing software. A dark original file always has the potential for increased noise as it is adjusted, and a light image may lose important detail in the highlights. AEB can help you to determine the best exposure for the situation. You won't use it all the time, but it can be very useful when the light in the scene varies in contrast or is complex in its dark and light values.

AEB is also important for a special digital editing technique that allows you to put multiple exposures together into one master to gain more tonal range from a scene. You can take the well-exposed highlights of one exposure and combine them with the better-detailed shadows of another (this works best with 1/2 stop bracketing). If you shot these different exposures with your camera on a tripod, they will line up exactly so that if you put the images on top of one another as layers using image-editing software, the different exposures are easy to combine. (You may even want to set the camera to continuous shooting—in this mode it will take the three photos for the AEB sequence and then stop.)

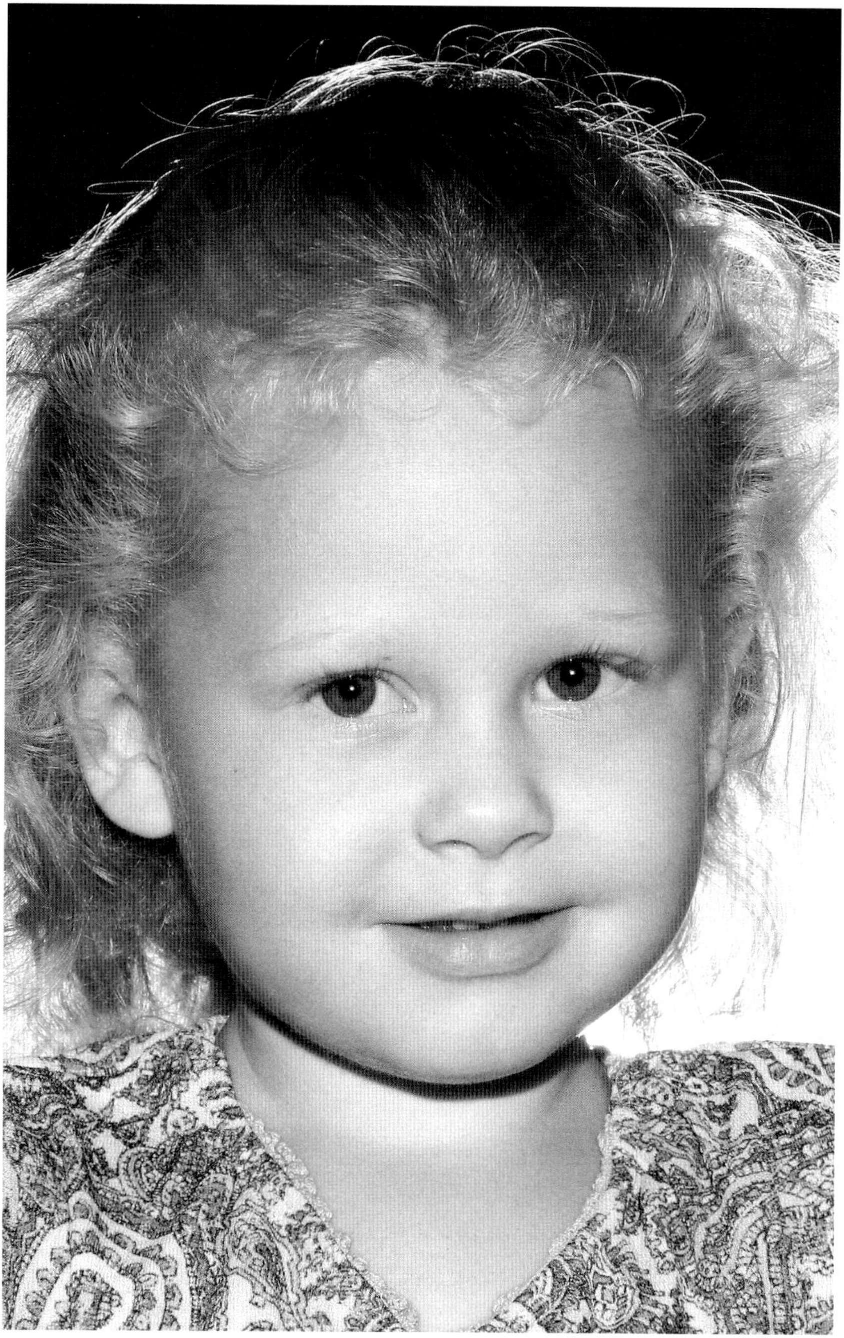

Flash

Electronic flash is not just a supplement for low light; it can also be a wonderful tool for creative photography. Flash is highly controllable, its color is precise, and the results are repeatable. However, the challenge is getting the right look, and many photographers shy away from using flash because they aren't happy with the results. This is because on-camera flash can be harsh and unflattering, and taking the flash off the camera used to be a complicated procedure with less than sure results. The EOS 20D's sophisticated flash system eliminates many of these concerns and, of course, the LCD Monitor gives instantaneous feedback. This alleviates the guesswork. With digital, you take a picture and you know immediately whether the lighting is right or not. You can then adjust the light level higher or lower, change the angle, soften the light, color it, and more. Just think of the possibilities:

Fill Flash — Fill in harsh shadows in all sorts of conditions and use the LCD Monitor to see exactly how well the fill flash is working. Often, you'll want to dial down an accessory flash to make its output more natural looking.

Off-Camera Flash — Putting a flash on a dedicated flash cord will allow you to move the flash to positions away from the camera and still have it work automatically. Using the LCD Monitor, you can see exactly what the effects are so you can move the flash up or down, left or right, for the best light and shadows on your subject.

The 20D helps you improve your flash photography through the use of Canon's improved E-TTL II flash system and the ability to review your flash photos in the LCD Monitor.

Close-Up Flash — This used to be a real problem, except for those willing to spend some time experimenting. Now you can see exactly what the flash is doing to the subject. This works fantastically well with off-camera flash, as you can "feather" the light (aim it so it doesn't hit the subject directly) to gain control over its strength and how it lights the area around the subject.

Multiple Flash — Modern flash systems have made exposure with multiple flash easier and more accurate. Plus, many manufacturers have created cordless systems. However, since the flash units are not on continuously, they can be hard to place so that they light the subject properly. Not anymore. With the 20D, it is easy to set up the flash, and then take a test shot. Does it look good, or not? Make changes if you need to. In addition, this camera lets you use certain EX-series flash units (and independent brands with the same capabilities) that offer wireless exposure control. This is a good way to learn how to master multiple flash set ups.

Colored Light — Many flashes look better with a slight warming filter on them, but that is not what this tip is about. With multiple light sources, you can attach colored filters (also called gels) to the various flashes so that different colors light different parts of the photo (this can be a very trendy look).

Balancing Mixed Lighting — Architectural and corporate photographers have long used added light to fill in dark areas of a scene so the scene looks less harsh. Now you can double-check the light balance on your subject using the LCD Monitor. You can even be sure the added light is the right color by attaching filters to the flash to mimic or match lights (such as a green filter to match fluorescents).

Flash Synchronization

The 20D is equipped with an electromagnetically timed, vertically traveling focal-plane shutter. One characteristic of focal-plane shutters is that, at shutter speeds faster than the flash sync speed, the entire surface of the sensor will not be exposed at the same time. The shutter then forms a slit, which exposes the sensor as it moves across it. If you use flash with a shutter speed that is higher than the maximum flash sync speed, you get only a partially exposed picture. However, at shutter speeds below the maximum, the whole sensor surface will be exposed at some point to accept the flash.

With the 20D, the maximum flash sync speed is 1/250 second (however, if you set the exposure to a speed faster than that in Tv or M modes when using flash, the camera will automatically reset the speed to 1/250). However, the camera does offer high-speed sync with EX-series flash units that allow flash at all shutter speeds (even 1/8000 second where, basically, the flash fires continuously as the slit goes down the sensor). High-speed synchronization must be activated on the flash unit itself and is indicated by an H symbol on the flash unit's LCD Panel—see the flash manual for specific information on using high-speed flash sync.

Guide Numbers

When shopping for a flash unit, it is helpful to compare guide numbers. A guide number (GN) is a simple way to state the power of the flash unit (it's computed as the product of aperture value and subject distance) and is usually included in the manufacturer's specifications for the unit. High numbers indicate more power, however, this is not a linear relationship. Guide numbers act a little like f/stops (because they are directly related to f/stops!)—e.g., 56 is half the power of 80, or 110 is twice the power of 80. Since guide numbers are expressed in feet and/or meters, distance is part of the guide number formula. Guide numbers are usually based on ISO 100 film, but this can vary, so check the film speed reference (and determine whether the GN was calculated using feet or meters) when comparing guide numbers for different units. If the flash units you are comparing have zoom-head diffusers, make sure you compare the guide numbers for similar zoom-head settings.

The built-in flash will pop up automatically in several of the Basic Zone exposure modes when the light is low.

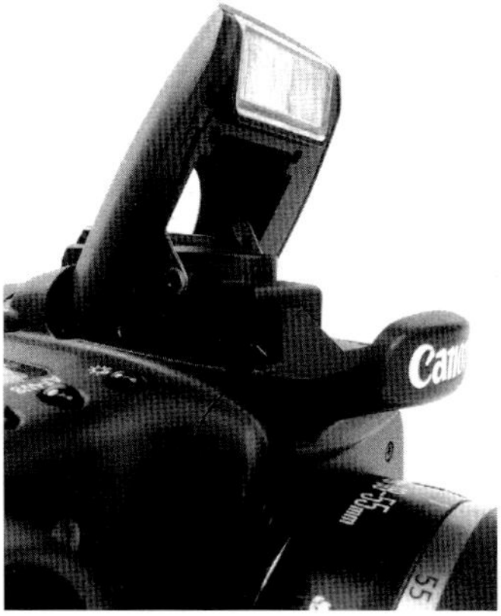

Built-in Flash

The on-board flash built into the pentaprism housing at the top of the camera pops up nearly an inch higher than the EOS 10D's flash, thereby reducing the chance of getting red-eye and minimizing problems with large lenses blocking the flash. The flash supports E-TTL II, covers a field of view up to a 17mm focal length and has a guide number of 43 (ISO 100, in feet). It is, like most built-in flash, not particularly high-powered, but its advantage is that it is always available and is very useful as fill-flash to modify ambient light. Unique to this flash and the 580EX, the flash sends color data to the camera's processor each time it fires. This helps the system measure many variables so that it can better maintain consistent color.

The flash pops up automatically in low light or backlit situations in the following Basic Zone exposure modes: Full Auto, Portrait, Close-Up, and Night Portrait. It will not activate in Landscape, Sports, or Flash Off modes. In the Creative Zone, you can choose to use the flash or not at any time. Just press the Flash button ⚡ on the upper left of the lens mount housing, and the flash will pop up. To turn it off, simply push the flash down.

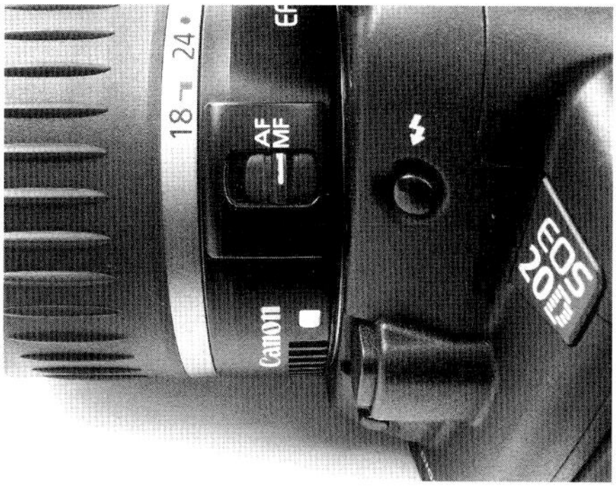

Press the Flash button at any time to raise the built-in flash.

There are some variations in how the Creative Zone exposure modes work with the built-in flash. Program is fully automatic. Tv can be used when you need a specific shutter speed. Av lets you set an aperture that the flash uses for its exposure and then the shutter speed influences how much of the "ambient" light (or natural light) will appear in the image. For M, you set the aperture for the flash then choose a shutter speed that is appropriate for your subject (you can use any shutter speed of 1/250 second and slower). For more information of using flash in the Creative Zone, see pages 129.

Flash Metering

The 20D uses an evaluative auto exposure system, called E-TTL II, with improved flash control over earlier models (it is based on the E-TTL II system introduced in the pro-level EOS-1D Mark II). To understand the 20D's flash metering, you need to understand how a flash works with a digital camera on automatic. The camera will cause the flash to fire twice for the exposure. First, a preflash is fired to analyze exposure, and then the flash fires during the actual exposure, creating the image. During the preflash, the camera's evaluative metering system measures the light reflected back from the subject. Once it senses that the light is sufficient, it cuts off the flash and takes the actual exposure with the same flash duration. The amount of flash hitting the subject is based on how long the flash is "on," so close subjects will receive shorter flash bursts than more distant subjects. This double flash system works quite well, but you may also find that it causes some subjects to react by closing their eyes during the real exposure. However, they will be well exposed!

You can lock the flash exposure when either the pop-up flash or an attached flash is turned on by pressing the FE (Flash Exposure) Lock button * (this is the same as the Exposure Lock button located on the upper right back of the camera). This causes the camera to emit a pre-flash so that it calculates the exposure before the shot. This also cancels the preflash that occurs immediately before the actual photograph (reducing the problem with people reacting to a preflash that occurs a split-second before the actual exposure).

To use this feature, turn the flash on, then lock focus on your subject by pressing the Shutter button halfway down. Next, aim the center of the viewfinder at the important part of the subject and press the FE Lock button (a * with the flash icon * will appear in the viewfinder). Now, reframe your composition and take the picture. FE Lock produces quite accurate flash exposures.

Using the same principle, you can make the flash weaker or stronger. Instead of pointing the viewfinder at the subject to set flash exposure, point it at something light in tone or a subject closer to the camera. That will cause the flash to give less exposure. For more light, aim the camera at something black or far away. With a little experimenting, and by reviewing the LCD Monitor, you can very quickly establish appropriate flash control for particular situations.

For the most control over flash, use the camera's Manual Exposure setting. Set an exposure that is correct overall for the scene then turn on the flash (flash exposure will still be E-TTL automatic.) The shutter speed (as long as it is 1/250 second or slower) controls the overall light from the scene (and the total exposure). The f/stop controls the exposure of the flash. So to a degree, you can make the overall scene lighter or darker by changing shutter speed, with no direct effect on the flash exposure (this does not work with high-speed flash).

Flash with Camera Exposure Modes

In the Basic Zones, you have no control over the flash. This means you have no say in when flash will be used for an exposure or how the exposure is controlled. The camera determines it all depending on how it senses the scene's light values. Either the light is dim or there is a strong backlight.

In the Creative Zones, you either pop up the built-in flash by pushing the Flash button or attach an EX Speedlite accessory flash unit and simply switch it to the ON position. The flash will then operate in the various Creative Zone modes as detailed below:

Program AE (P)

Flash photography can be used for any photo where supplementary light is needed. All you have to do is turn on the flash unit—the camera does the rest automatically. Speedlite EX flash units should be switched to E-TTL and the ready light should be on, indicating that the flash is ready to fire. While shooting, you must pay attention to the flash symbol in the viewfinder to be sure that the flash is charged when you are ready to take your picture. The 20D sets flash synchronization shutter speeds of 1/60–1/250 second automatically in P mode and also selects the correct aperture. When the flash is turned on, any Program shift that has been set will be canceled.

Shutter-Priority AE (Tv)

This mode is a good choice in situations where you want to control the shutter speed when you are also using flash. In Tv mode, you set the shutter speed before or after a dedicated accessory flash is turned on. All shutter speeds between 1/250 second and 30 seconds will synchronize with the flash. With E-TTL Flash in Tv mode, synchronization with longer shutter speeds is a creative choice that allows you to control the ambient-light background exposure. A portrait of a person at dusk in front of a building with its lights on shot with conventional TTL flash would illuminate the person correctly but would cause the background to go dark. However, using Tv mode, you can control the exposure of the background by changing the shutter speed. (A tripod is recommended to keep the camera stable during long exposures).

Aperture-Priority AE (Av)

Using this mode lets you balance the flash with existing light, and it allows you to control depth of field in the composition. By selecting the aperture, you are also able to influence the range of the flash. The aperture can be selected by turning the Main Dial and watching the flash's LCD Panel until the desired range appears. Then the camera calculates the lighting conditions and automatically sets the correct flash shutter speed for the ambient light.

Manual Exposure (M)

Going Manual gives you the most choices in modifying exposure. The photographer who prefers to adjust everything manually can determine the relationship of ambient light and electronic flash by setting both the aperture and shutter speed. Any aperture on the lens and all shutter speeds between 1/250 second and 30 seconds can be used. If a shutter speed above the normal flash sync speed is set, the 20D switches automatically to 1/250 second to prevent partial exposure of the sensor.

M mode also offers a number of creative possibilities for using flash in connection with long shutter speeds. You could use zooming effects with smeared background and a sharply rendered main subject, or take photographs of objects in motion with a sharp "flash core" and indistinct outlines.

Red-Eye Reduction

The 20D does offer a red-eye reduction feature for flash exposures. In low-light conditions when the flash is close to the axis of the lens (which it is with built-in flash, although the 20D's flash pops up higher than most), the flash will reflect back from the retina of peoples' eyes (because their pupils are wide). This appears as "red-eye" in the photo. You can reduce the chances of red-eye appearing with an off-camera flash or by having the person look at a bright light before shooting.

The red-eye reduction feature of a camera is designed to cause the pupils of your subject to contract. On many cameras this is of questionable value because the flash fires a burst of light before the actual exposure. This often causes less than flattering expressions from your subject. The 20D, on the other hand, uses a continuous light from a bulb next to the handgrip, just below the Shutter button (you do have to be careful not to block it with your fingers), which helps the subject pose with better expressions. Red-eye reduction is set in the Shooting menu under *Red-eye On/Off*.

Canon Speedlite EX Flash Units

Canon offers a range of accessory flash units, called Speedlites, in the EOS system. While Canon Speedlites don't replace studio strobes, they are remarkably versatile. These highly portable flash units can be mounted in the camera's hot shoe or used off camera with a dedicated cord. The 20D is compatible with the EX-series of Speedlites. The EX-series flash units range in power from the Speedlite 580EX, which has a maximum GN of 190 (ISO 100, in feet), to the small and compact Speedlite 220EX, which has a GN of 72 (ISO 100, in feet). Speedlite EX-series flash units offer a wide range of features to expand your creativity. These are designed to work with the camera's microprocessor to take advantage of E-TTL exposure control, which extends the abilities of the 20D considerably.

I also strongly recommend Canon's Off-Camera Shoe Cord 2, an extension cord for your flash. With this cord, the flash can be moved away from the camera for more interesting light and shadow. You can aim light from the side or top of a close-up subject for variations in contrast and color. If you find that you get an overexposed subject, rather than dialing down the flash (which can be done on certain flash units), just aim the flash a little away from the subject so it doesn't get hit so directly by the light. That is often a quick fix for overexposure of close-ups.

Canon Speedlite 580EX

This top-of-the-line flash unit offers outstanding range and features adapted to digital cameras. It has many features in common with the 550EX but is slightly more powerful, has a faster recycling time, and is a more compact. The tilt/swivel zoom head on the 580EX covers focal lengths from 14mm to 105mm, and it swivels a full 180° in either direction. The zoom positions (which correspond to the focal lengths 24, 28, 35, 50, 70, 80, and 105mm) can be set manually or automatically (the flash reflector zooms with the lens). In addition, this flash "knows" what size sensor is used with a digital SLR and will vary its zoom accordingly. With the built-in retractable diffuser in place, the flash coverage is wide enough for a 14mm lens. It provides a high flash output with a GN of 190 (ISO 100, in feet) when the zoom head is positioned at 105mm. The guide number decreases as the angular coverage increases for shorter focal lengths, but is still quite high with a GN of 145 at 50mm, or GN 103 at 28mm.

The large, illuminated LCD Panel on the 580EX provides clear information on all settings: flash function, reflector position, working aperture, and flash range in feet or meters. The flash also includes a new Select Dial for easier selection of these settings. When you press the 20D's Depth-of-Field Preview button (on lower left of the lens mount housing), a one-second burst of light is emitted. This modeling flash allows you to judge the effect of the flash. The 580EX also has 13 user-defined custom settings that are totally independent of the camera's custom functions; for more information, see the flash manual. When using multiple flashes, the 580EX can be used either as a master flash or a slave unit.

Canon Speedlite 550EX

This model provides high performance with a GN of 182 (ISO 100, in feet) when the zoom head is positioned at 105mm. The guide number decreases as the angular coverage increases for wider angle lenses, but is still quite high with a GN of 139 at 50mm or GN 99 at 28mm. The tilt/swivel zoom head on the 550EX covers focal lengths from 24mm to 105mm. The zoom positions (which correspond to the focal lengths 24, 28, 35,

50, 70, 80, and 105mm) can be set manually or automatically (the flash reflector zooms with the lens). With the built-in retractable diffuser in place, the flash coverage is wide enough for a 17mm lens.

Just like the 580EX, the 550EX features a large, illuminated LCD Panel that provides clear information on all settings. It also works like the 580EX when you press the Depth-of-Field Preview button to judge the effect of your flash. This unit also has six custom settings that can be defined by the user. When using multiple flash units, the 550EX can be used either as a master flash or a slave unit.

Canon Speedlite 420EX

The 420EX is less complicated, more compact, and less expensive than the top models. It offers E-TTL flash control, wireless E-TTL operation, and high-speed synchronization. The 420EX flash unit provides high performance with a GN of 138 (ISO 100, in feet) with the zoom reflector set for 105mm (somewhat weaker than the 550EX, but still quite powerful). The tilt/swivel zoom reflector covers focal lengths from 24 to 105mm. The zoom head operates automatically for focal lengths of 24, 28, 35, 50, 70 and 105mm. The setting for wireless E-TTL is made on the flash foot. When using multiple flashes, the 420EX can be used as a slave unit, but not as a master flash.

Other Speedlites

Other Speedlite EX flash units include the Speedlite 220EX and 380EX. The 220EX is an economy alternative EX-series flash. The Speedlite 380EX is a discontinued model, but is still a good choice if you can find one on the used market. Both of these models offer E-TTL flash and high-speed sync but do not offer wireless TTL flash or exposure bracketing.

There are also two specialized flash units for close-up photography that work well with the EOS 20D: the Macro Twin Lite MT-24EX and the Macro Ring Lite MR-14EX. They provide direct light on the subject.

Macro Twin Lite MT-24EX

The MT-24EX uses two small flashes affixed to a ring that attaches to the lens. These can be adjusted to different positions to alter the light and can be used at different strengths so one can be used as a main light and the other as a fill light. If both flash tubes are switched on, they produce a GN of 72 (ISO 100, in feet), and when used individually the guide number is 36. It does an exceptional job with directional lighting in macro shooting.

Macro Ring Lite MR-14EX

The MR-14EX has a GN of 46 (ISO 100, in feet) and both flash tubes can be independently adjusted in 13 steps from 1:8 to 8:1. It is a flash that encircles the lens and provides illumination on axis with it. This results in nearly shadowless photos (the shadow falls behind the subject compared to the lens position, though there will be shadow effects along curved edges). This flash is often used by photographers who want to show all the fine detail and color in a subject. It cannot be used for varied light and shadow effects. This flash is commonly used in medical and dental photography so that important details are not obscured by shadows.

Note: The power pack of both of these specialized flash units fits into the flash shoe of the camera. In addition, both macro flash units offer the same technical features as the 550EX, including E-TTL operation, wireless E-TTL flash, and high-speed synchronization among others. The MT-24EX models can also be used for wireless E-TTL flash.

Note: When the 20D is used with older system flash units (such as the EZ series), the flash unit must be set to manual, and TTL will not function. For this reason, Canon EX Speedlite system flash units are recommended primarily for use with the camera.

Bounce Flash

Direct flash can often be harsh and unflattering, causing heavy shadows behind the subject or underneath features such as eyebrows and bangs. Bouncing the flash softens the light and creates a more natural-looking light effect. The Canon Speedlite 580EX, 550EX, and 420EX accessory flash units feature heads that are designed to tilt so that a shoe-mounted flash can be aimed at the ceiling to produce soft, even lighting. The 580EX and 550EX also swivel (the 580EX 180° in both directions) so the light can be bounced off something to the side of the camera (a wall or reflector). However, the ceiling or wall must be white or neutral gray, or it may cause an undesirable color cast in the finished photo.

Wireless E-TTL Flash

With the wireless E-TTL feature, you can use up to three groups of Speedlite 580EXs, 550Exs, or 420EXs for more natural lighting or emphasis (the number of flash groups is limited to three, but the number of actual flash units is unlimited). The master unit and the camera control the exposure. A switch on the back of the foot of the 580EX and 550EX allows you to select whether the flash will be used as a master or a slave flash in the set up. The 420EX can only be used as a slave unit. Other wireless flash options include the Speedlite infrared transmitter (ST-E2), or the Macro Twin Lite MT-24EX.

To operate wireless TTL, a Speedlite 580EX or 550EX is mounted in the flash shoe on the camera. The switch on the unit's foot should be set so that it functions as a master unit, and slave units are set up in the surrounding area. The light ratio of slave units can be varied manually or automatically. With E-TTL (wireless) control several different Speedlite 420EXs, 550EXs, and 580EXs can be controlled at once.

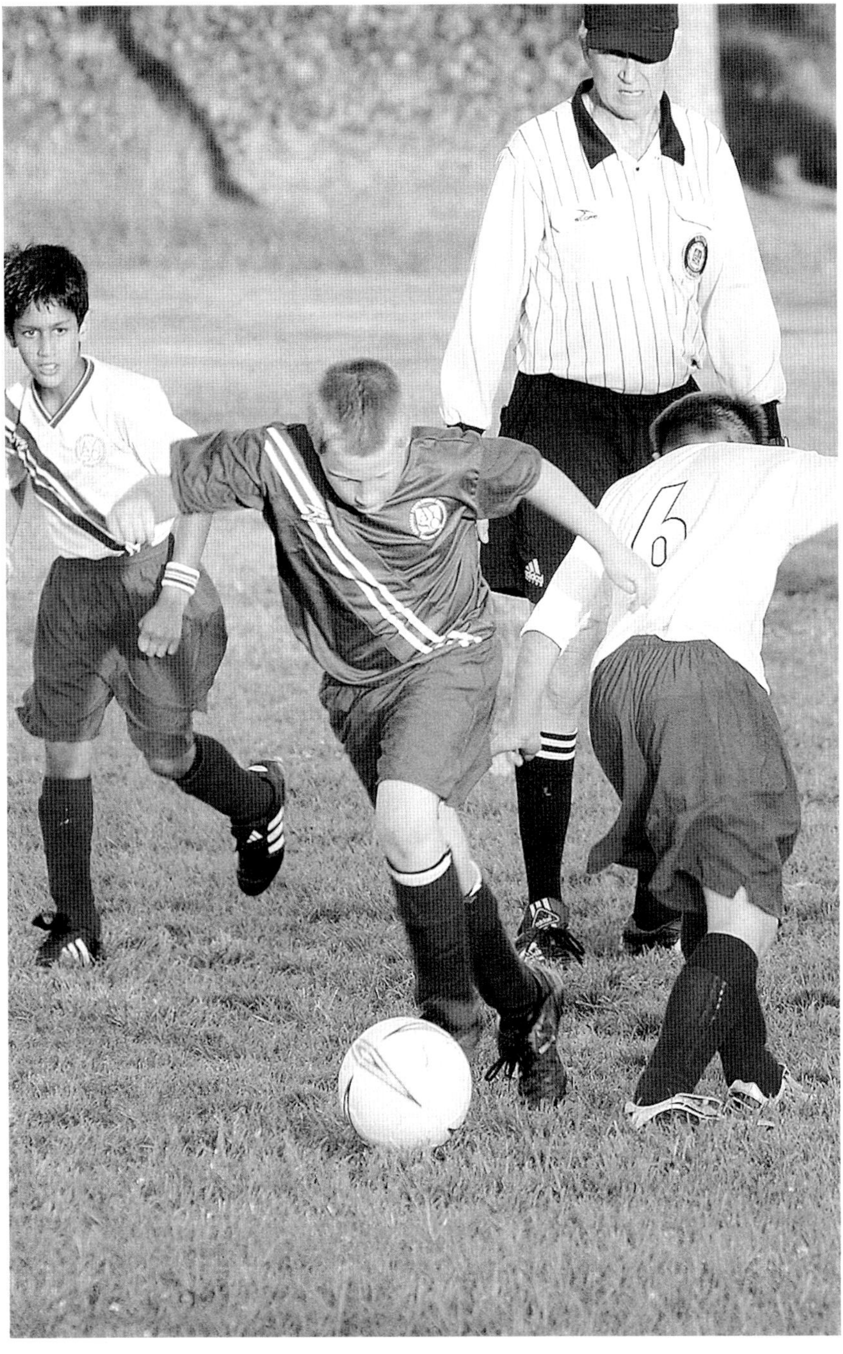

Lenses and Accessories

The 20D belongs to an extensive family of Canon EOS compatible equipment, including lenses, flashes, and other accessories. With this wide range of available options, you could expand the capabilities of your camera quite easily should you want to. Canon has long had an excellent reputation for its lenses, and several independent manufacturers offer quality Canon compatible lenses as well.

The 20D can use both Canon EF and EF-S lenses, ranging from wide-angle to tele-zoom, as well as single-focal-length lenses, from very wide to extreme telephoto. Keep in mind that both the widest angle and the farthest zoom are multiplied by the 20D's 1.6x magnification factor (see page 40). The EF 14mm f/2.8L lens, for example, is a super-wide lens with a 35mm camera, but offers the 35mm-format equivalent of a 22mm wide-angle lens when attached to the EOS 20D—wide, but not super-wide. On the other hand, put a 400mm lens on the camera and you get the equivalent of a 640mm telephoto—a big boost with no change in aperture (be sure to use a tripod for these focal lengths)!

Choosing Lenses

The focal length and design of a lens will have a huge affect on how you photograph. The correct lens will make photography a joy; the wrong one will make you leave the camera at home. One approach for choosing a lens is to determine if

Interchangeable lenses for digital SLRs offer versatility. You can get extremely close to your subject with close-up lenses, or you can shoot from a distance and still capture detailed action with telephotos.

you are frustrated with your current lenses. Do you constantly want to see more of the scene than the lens will allow? Then consider a wider-angle lens. Or maybe the subject is too small in your photos. Then look into acquiring a zoom or telephoto lens.

Certain subjects lend themselves to specific focal lengths. Wildlife and sports action are best photographed using focal lengths of 300mm or more, although nearby action can be managed with 200mm. Portraits look great when shot with focal lengths between 80 and 100mm. Interiors often demand wide-angle lenses such as 20 or 24mm. Many people also like wide-angles for landscapes, but telephotos can come in handy for distant scenes. Close-ups can be shot with nearly any focal length, though skittish subjects such as butterflies might need a rather long lens.

These focal lengths are traditional 35mm equivalents, because most people who know photography are familiar with these measurements. However, on most digital cameras the standard 35mm focal lengths do not act the way they did with film. That is because these digital sensors are smaller than a frame of 35mm film, so they crop the area seen by the lens, essentially creating a different format. Effectively, this magnifies the subject within the image area of the 20D and results in the lens acting as if it has been multiplied by a factor of 1.6 compared to 35mm film cameras.

Note: This is exactly the same thing that happens when one focal length is used with different sized film formats. For example, a 50mm lens is considered a mid-range focal length for 35mm, but it would be a wide-angle for medium format cameras.

This is great news for the photographer who needs long focal lengths for wildlife or sports. A standard 300mm lens for 35mm film now acts like a 480mm lens on the 20D. You get a long focal length in a smaller lens, often with a wider maximum f/stop, and with a much lower price tag. But this news is tough for people who need wide-angles, since the width of what the digital camera sees is significantly cropped in comparison to what a 35mm camera would see using the same lens. You will need lenses with shorter focal lengths to see the same amount of wide-angle you may have been used to with film.

Zoom vs. Prime Lenses

When zoom lenses first came on the market, they were not even close to a single-focal-length lens in sharpness, color rendition, or contrast. Today, you can get superb image quality from either type. There are some important differences, though. The biggest is maximum f/stop.

Zoom lenses are rarely as fast (e.g. rarely have as big a maximum aperture) as single-focal-length, or prime, lenses. A 28-200mm zoom, for example, might have a maximum aperture at 200mm of f/5.6, yet a single-focal-length lens might be f/4 or even f/2.8. When zoom lenses come close to a single-focal-length lens in f/stops, they are usually considerably bigger and more expensive than the single-focal-length lens. Of course, they also offer a whole range of focal lengths, which a single-focal-length lens cannot do. There is no question that zoom lenses are versatile.

EF-Series Lenses

Canon EF lenses include some unique technologies. Canon pioneered the use of tiny autofocus motors in its lenses. In order to focus swiftly, the focusing elements within the lens need to move with quick precision. Canon developed the lens-based ultrasonic motor for this purpose. This technology makes the lens motor spin with ultrasonic oscillation energy instead of the conventional drive-train system (which tends to be noisy). This allows lenses to autofocus nearly instantly and with no noise (plus it uses less battery power than traditional systems). Canon lenses that utilize this motor are labeled USM (lower-priced Canon lenses have small motors in the lenses too, but they don't use USM technology, and can be slower and noisier).

Canon was also a pioneer in the use of image-stabilizing technologies. IS (Image Stabilizer) lenses use sophisticated motors and sensors to adapt to slight movement during exposure. It's pretty amazing—the lens actually has vibration-detecting gyro stabilizers that move a special image-stabilizing lens group in response to movement of the lens. This dampens movement that occurs from handholding a camera and allows much slower shutter speeds to be used. IS also allows big telephoto lenses (such as the EF 500mm IS lens) to be used on tripods that are lighter than would normally be used with non IS telephoto lenses.

The IS technology is part of many zoom lenses, and does a great job overall. However, IS lenses in the mid-focal length ranges have tended to be slower zooms matched against single-focal-length lenses. For example, compare the EF 28–135mm f/3.5–5.6 IS lens to the EF 85mm f/1.8. The former has a great zoom range, but allows less light at maximum aperture. At 85mm (a good focal length for people), the EF 28–135mm is an f/4 lens, more than two stops slower than the f/1.8 single-focal-length lens when both are shot "wide-open" (typical of low light situations). While you could make up that two stops in "handholdability" due to the IS technology, that also means you must use two full shutter speeds slower, which can be a real problem in stopping subject movement.

EF-S Series Lenses

EF lenses are the standard lenses for all Canon EOS cameras. EF-S lenses are small, compact lenses designed to only cover the format size of a small-format digital camera. They were introduced with the EF-S 18–55mm lens packaged with the EOS Digital Rebel. They cannot be used with film EOS cameras, the EOS-1Ds Mark II, or the EOS-1D Mark II, because the image area for each of those cameras is larger than that of the 20D's sensor.

With the introduction of the 20D, Canon also introduced two new EF-S lenses. The EF-S 17–85mm f/4–5.6 IS USM is an image stabilized zoom that offers the 35mm equivalent of approximately 28–135mm in a very compact package. The EF-S 10–22mm f/3.5–4.5 USM zoom brings an excellent wide-angle range to the 20D by offering the equivalent of 16–35mm on a full-size 35mm frame.

L-Series Lenses

Canon's L-series lenses use special optical technologies for high-quality lens correction. These include low-dispersion glass, fluorite elements, and aspherical designs. UD (ultra-low dispersion) glass is used in L-series telephoto lenses to minimize chromatic aberration, a common problem for telephoto lens designers. Chromatic aberration occurs when the lens can't focus all colors equally at the same point on the sensor (as well as on the film in a traditional camera). This results in less sharpness and a lot less contrast. Low-dispersion glass focuses colors more equally for sharper, crisper images.

Fluorite elements are even more effective (though more expensive) and have the corrective power of two UD lens elements. Aspherical designs are used with wide-angle and mid-focal length lenses to correct the challenges of spherical aberration in such focal lengths. Spherical aberration is a problem caused by lens elements with extreme curvature (usually found in wide-angle and wide-angle zoom lenses). Glass tends to focus light differently through different parts of such a lens, causing a slight, overall softening of the image even though the lens is focused sharply. Aspherical lenses use a special design that compensates for this optical defect.

DO-Series Lenses

A relatively recent Canon optical design is the DO, which stands for diffractive optic. This is a very promising technology that significantly reduces the size and weight of a lens, and therefore is especially useful for big telephotos and zooms. Yet, the lens quality is unchanged. The first two lenses produced by

Canon in this series are a 400mm pro lens that is only two-thirds the size and weight of the equivalent standard lens, and a 70-300mm IS lens that offers a great focal length range while including image stabilization.

Macro and Tilt-Shift Lenses

Canon also makes some specialized lenses. Macro lenses are single-focal-length lenses optimized for high sharpness throughout their focus range, from very close (1:1 or 1:2) magnifications to infinity. These lenses range from 50mm to 180mm.

Tilt-shift lenses are unique lenses that shift up and down or tilt toward or away from the subject. They mimic the controls of a view camera. Shift lets the photographer keep the back of the camera parallel to the scene and move the lens to get a tall subject into the composition – this keeps vertical lines vertical and is extremely valuable for architectural photographers. Tilt changes the plane of focus so that sharpness can be changed without changing the f/stop. Focus can be extended from near to far by tilting the lens toward the subject, or sharpness can be limited by tilting the lens away from the subject (which has lately been a trendy advertising photography technique).

Independent Lens Brands

Independent lens manufacturers also make some excellent lenses that fit the 20D. I've seen quite a range in capabilities from these lenses. Some include low-dispersion glass and are stunningly sharp. Others may not match the best Canon lenses, but offer features (such as focal length range or a great price) that make them worth considering. To a degree, you do get what you pay for. A low-priced Canon lens compared to a low-priced independent lens probably won't be much different. On the other hand, the high level of engineering and construction found on a Canon L-series lens can be difficult to match.

Filters and Close-Up Lenses

Many people these days assume that filters aren't needed for digital photography because adjustments for color and light can be made in the computer. By no means are filters obsolete! They actually save a substantial amount of work in the digital darkroom by allowing you to capture the desired color and tonalities for your image right from the start. Even if you can do certain things in the computer, why take the time if you can do it more efficiently while shooting?

Of course, the LCD monitor comes in handy once again. By using it, you can assist yourself in getting the best from your filters. If you aren't sure how a filter works, you can simply try it and see the results immediately on the monitor. This is like using a Polaroid, only better, because you need no extra gear. Just take the shot, review it, and make adjustments to the exposure or white balance to help the filter do its job. If a picture doesn't come out the way you would like, you can discard and retake it right away.

Attaching filters to the camera depends entirely on your lenses. Usually, a properly sized filter can either be screwed directly onto a lens or fit into a holder that screws onto the front of the lens. There are adapters to make a given size filter fit several lenses, but the filter must cover the lens from edge to edge or it will cause dark corners in the photo (vignetting). A photographer may even hold a filter over the lens with his or her hand. There are a number of different types of filters that perform different tasks.

Polarizers

This important outdoor filter should be in every camera bag. Its effects cannot be exactly duplicated with software because it actually affects the way light is perceived by the sensor.

A polarizer darkens skies at 90 degrees to the sun (this is a variable effect), reduces glare (which will often make colors look better), removes reflections, and increases saturation. While you can darken skies in the computer, the polarizer reduces the amount of work you have to perform in the digital darkroom. This filter will rotate in its mount, and as it rotates, the strength of the effect changes. While linear polarizers often have the strongest effect, they can cause problems with exposure, and often prevent the camera from autofocusing. Consequently, you are safer using a circular polarizer with the 20D.

Neutral Density Gray Filters

Called ND filters, this type is a helpful accessory. ND filters simply reduce the light coming through the lens. These filters come in different strengths, each reducing different quantities of light. They give additional exposure options under bright conditions, such as a beach or snow (where a filter with a strength of 4x is often appropriate). If you like the effects when slow shutter speeds are used with moving subjects, a strong neutral density filter (such as 8x) usually works well. Of course, the great advantage of the digital camera, again, is that you can see the effects of slow shutter speeds immediately on the LCD monitor so you can modify your exposure for the best possible effect.

Graduated Neutral Density Filters

Many photographers consider this filter an essential tool. It is half clear and half dark (gray). It is used to reduce bright areas (such as sky) in tone, while not affecting darker areas (such as the ground). The computer can mimic its effects, but you may not be able to recreate the scene you wanted. A digital camera's sensor can only respond to a certain range of brightness at any given exposure, and if a part of the scene is too bright compared to the overall exposure, detail will be washed out and no amount of work in the computer will bring it back.

UV and Skylight Filters

Though many amateur photographers buy these, pros rarely use them. The idea behind them is to give protection to the front of the lens, but they do very little visually. Still, they can be useful when photographing under such conditions as strong wind, rain, blowing sand, or going through brush.

If you do use a filter for lens protection, a high quality filter is best. A cheap filter can degrade the image quality of the lens. Remember that the manufacturer made the lens/sensor combination with very strict tolerances. A protective filter needs to be literally invisible, and only high-quality filters can guarantee that.

Close-Up Lenses

Close-up photography is a striking and unique way to capture a scene. Most of the photographs we see on a day-to-day basis are not close-ups, making those that do make their way to our eyes all the more noticeable. It is surprising to me that many photographers think the only way to shoot close-ups is with a macro lens. The following are four of the most common close-up options:

1. ***Close-focusing zoom lenses with a macro or close-focus feature***
   Most zoom lenses allow you to focus up-close without accessories, although focal-length choices may become limited when using the close-focus feature. These lenses are an easy and effective way to start shooting close-ups. Keep in mind, however, that even though these may say they have a macro setting, it is really just a close-focus setting and not a true macro as described below in option four.

2. ***Close-up accessory lenses***
   You can buy lenses that screw onto the front of your lens to allow it to focus even closer. The advantage is that you now have the whole range of zoom focal lengths available and there are no exposure corrections. Close-up filters can do this, but the image quality is not great. More expensive achromatic accessory lenses (highly-corrected, multi-element lenses) do a superb job with close-up work, but their quality is limited by the original lens.

3. ***Extension tubes***
   Extension tubes fit in between the lens and the camera body of an SLR. This allows the lens to focus much closer than it could normally. Extension tubes are designed to work with all lenses for your camera (although older exten-

sion tubes won't always match some of the new lenses made specifically for digital cameras). Be aware that extension tubes do cause a loss of light.

4. ***Macro lenses***
   Though relatively expensive, macro lenses are designed for superb sharpness at all distances and will focus from mere inches to infinity. In addition, they are typically very sharp at all f/stops.

Sharpness is a big issue with close-ups, and this is not simply a matter of buying a well-designed macro lens. The other close-up options can also give superbly sharp images. Sharpness problems usually result from three factors: limited depth of field, incorrect focus placement, and camera movement.

The closer you get to a subject, the shallower depth of field becomes. You can stop your lens down as far as it will go for more depth of field, or use a lens with a wider angle, but depth of field will still be limited. Because of this, it is critical to be sure focus is placed correctly on the subject. If the back of an insect is sharp but its eyes aren't, the photo will appear to have a focus problem. At these close distances, every detail counts. If only half of the flower petals are in focus, the overall photo will not look sharp. Autofocus up close can be a real problem with critical focus placement because the camera will often focus on the wrong part of the photo.

Of course, you can review your photo on the LCD monitor to be sure the focus is correct before leaving your subject. You can also try manual focus. One technique is to focus the lens at a reasonable distance, then move the camera toward and away from the subject as you watch it go in and out of focus. This can really help, but still, you may find that taking multiple photos is the best way to guarantee proper focus at these close distances. Another good technique is to shoot on the continuous drive mode and fire multiple photos. You will often find at least one shot with the critical part of your subject in focus. This is a great technique when you are handholding and when you want to capture moving subjects.

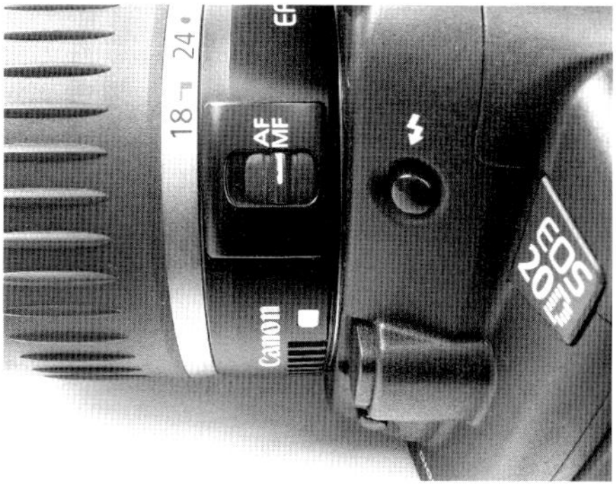

The Lens Release button allows you to change lenses as needed. It is located on front of the camera, on the left side of the lens mount housing below the Flash button.

When you are focusing close, even slight movement can shift the camera dramatically in relationship to the subject. The way to help correct this is to use a high shutter speed or put the camera on a tripod. Two advantages to using a digital camera during close-up work are the ability to check the image to see if you are having camera movement problems, as well as the ability to change ISO settings from picture to picture to enable a faster shutter speed if you deem it necessary.

The best looking close-up images will often be ones that allow the subject to contrast with its background, making it stand out and adding some drama to the photo. There are three important contrast options to keep in mind. They apply to any photograph where you want the subject to stand out, but they can be easily applied to close-up subjects where a slight movement of the camera can totally change the background.

There are three important contrast options to keep in mind:

1. ***Tonal or brightness contrasts***
   Look for a background that is darker or lighter than your close-up subject. This may mean a small adjustment in camera position. Backlight is excellent for this since it offers bright edges on your subject with lots of dark shadows behind it.

2. ***Color contrasts***
   Color contrast is a great way of making your subject stand out from the background. Flowers are popular close-up

subjects and, with their bright colors, they are perfect candidates for this type of contrast. Just look for a background that is either a completely different color (such as green grass behind red flowers) or a different saturation of color (such as a bright green bug against dark green grass).

3. ***Sharpness contrast***
   One of the best close-up techniques is to work with the inherent limit in depth of field and deliberately set a sharp subject against an out-of-focus background or foreground. Look at the distance between your subject and its surroundings. How close are other objects to your subject? Move to a different angle so that distractions are not conflicting with the edges of your subject. Try different f/stops to change the look of an out-of-focus background or foreground.

Tripods and Camera Support

A successful approach to getting the most from a digital camera is to be aware that camera movement can affect sharpness and tonal brilliance in an image. Even slight movement during the exposure can cause the loss of fine details and the blurring of highlights. These effects are especially glaring when you compare an affected image to a photo that has no motion problems. In addition, affected images will not enlarge well.

You must minimize camera movement in order to maximize the capabilities of your lens and sensor. A steady hold on the camera is a start. Fast shutter speeds, as well as the use of flash, help to ensure sharp photos, although you can get away with slower shutter speeds when using wider-angle lenses. However, when shutter speeds go down, it is advisable to use a camera-stabilizing device. Tripods, beanbags, monopods, mini-tripods, shoulder stocks, clamps, and more all help. Many photographers carry a small beanbag or a clamp pod with their camera equipment for those situations where the camera needs support but a tripod isn't available.

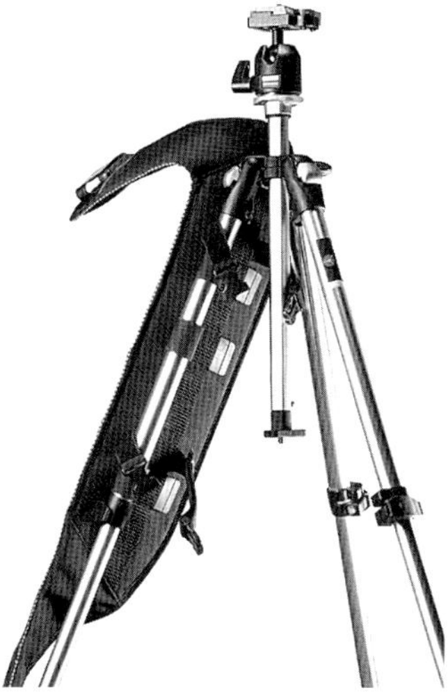

A sturdy tripod will eliminate camera movement, giving you the opportunity to shoot sharper photos that will enlarge better. © Bogen Imaging Inc.

Check your local camera store for the variety of stabilizing equipment. A good tripod is an excellent investment. When buying a tripod, extend it all the way to see how easy it is to open, then lean on it to see how stiff it is. Both aluminum and carbon fiber tripods offer great rigidity. Carbon fiber is much lighter, but also more expensive.

The head is a very important part of the tripod and may be sold separately. There are two basic types for still photography: the ball head and the pan-and-tilt head. Both designs are capable of solid support and both have their passionate advocates. The biggest difference between them is how you loosen the controls and adjust the camera. Try both and see which seems to work better for you. Be sure to do this with a camera on the tripod because that added weight changes how the head works.

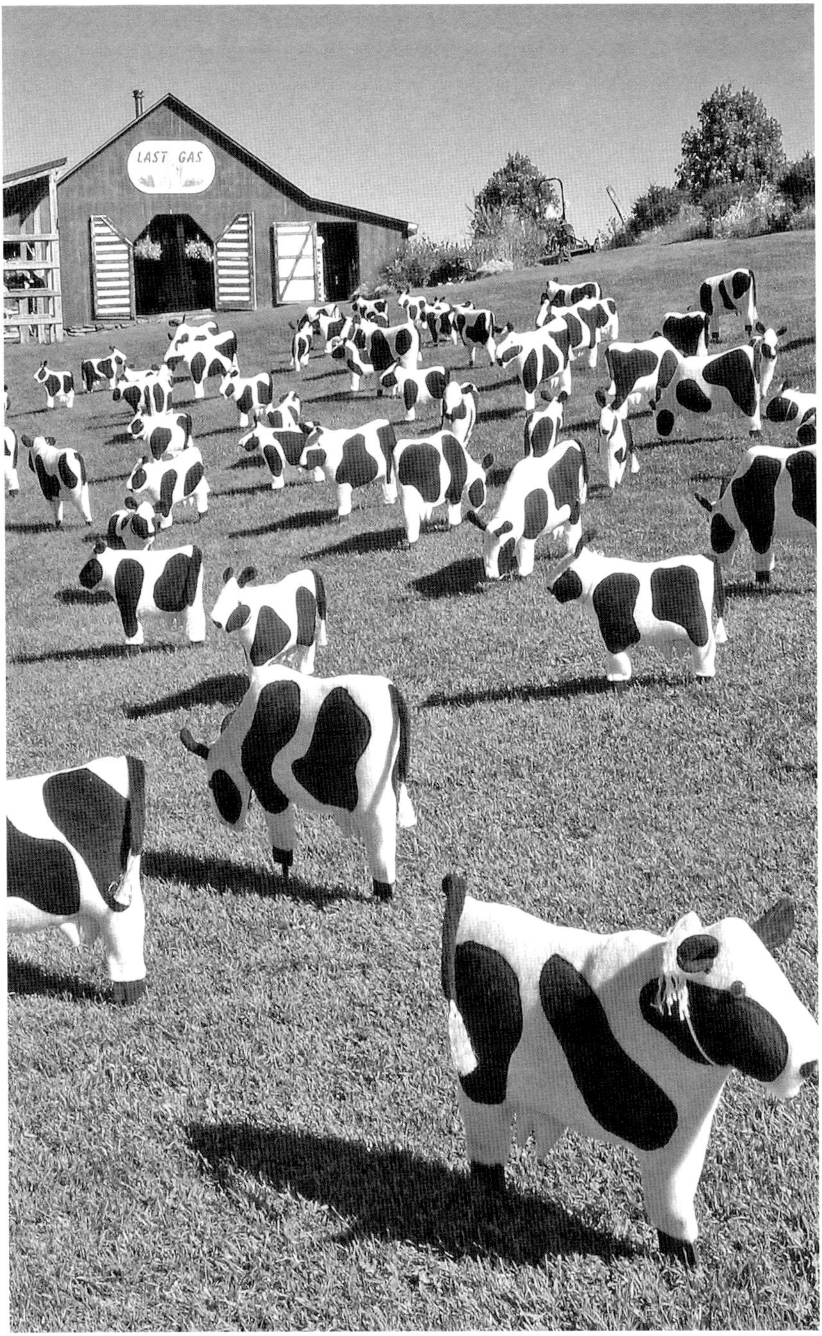
LAST GAS

Working with the Computer

Camera to Computer

There are two main ways of duplicating digital files from the memory card into the computer. One way is to insert the card into an accessory known as a card reader. Card readers connect to your computer through the USB or FireWire ports and can remain plugged in and ready to download your pictures. The second way is to download images directly from the 20D using a USB interface cable (included with the camera at the time of purchase).

FireWire, if you have that capability on your computer, is faster than USB, which has two types: USB 1.0 and 2.0. Older computers and card readers will have the 1.0 version, but new devices are most likely 2.0. This new version of USB is much faster than the old.

The advantage of downloading directly from the camera is that you don't need to buy a card reader. However, there are some distinct disadvantages. For one, cameras generally download much more slowly than card readers (given the same connections). Plus, a camera has to be unplugged from the computer after each use (the card reader can be left attached). As well as these drawbacks, downloading directly from a camera uses its battery power in making the transfer (or you need to plug it into AC power).

You can connect and print directly from your 20D if your printer is compatible with the PictBridge standard, bypassing the process of downloading picture files into your computer.

The Card Reader

A card reader can be purchased at most electronics stores. There are several different types, including single-card readers that read only one particular type of memory card, or multi-readers that are able to utilize several different kinds of cards. The latter is important with the 20D only if you have several cameras using different memory card types. After your card reader is connected to your computer, remove the memory card from your camera and put it into the appropriate slot in your card reader.

The card will usually show up as an additional drive on your computer (on Windows XP and Mac OS IX and X operating systems—for other versions you may have to install the drivers that come with the card reader). When the computer recognizes the card, it may also give instructions for downloading. You may want to follow these instructions if you are unsure about opening and moving the files yourself, but this is much slower than simply selecting your files and dragging them to where you want them.

Card readers can also be used with laptops, though PC card adapters may be more convenient when you're on the move. As long as your laptop has a PC card slot, all you need is a PC card adapter for your particular type of memory card. Insert the memory card into the PC adapter, then insert the PC adapter into your laptop's PC card slot. The computer will recognize this as a new drive, and then you can drag and drop images from the card to the hard drive. The latest PC card adapter models tend to be faster but are also more expensive.

Working with Files

How do you edit and file your digital photos so that they are accessible and easy to use? To start, it helps to create folders specific to groups of images (i.e., XYZ Corporation, Portraits, Downtown Fair, Acme Equipment Demo, etc.). You can organize your photo folders alphabetically or by date inside a "parent" folder.

Be sure to edit your photos and remove extraneous shots. Unwanted photos stored on your computer waste storage space on your hard drive, so you should store only the ones you intend to keep. Take a moment and review your pictures while the card is still in the camera. Erase the ones you don't want, and download the rest. You can also delete photos once downloaded to the computer by using a browser program (described below)

Here's how I deal with digital camera files. I use a memory card reader that shows up as a drive on my computer. Using the computer's file system, I open the memory card as a window or open folder (this is the same basic view on Windows and Mac computers) showing the images in the appropriate folder. I then open another window or folder on the computer's hard drive, and create a new subfolder labeled to signify the photographs on the memory card, such as *Place, Topic, Date*. I also create all of these folders in a specific location on my hard drive—I use a folder called Digital Images. Then inside that, folders by year, then the individual shoots (you could use locations, months, whatever works for you). This is really no different than setting up an office filing cabinet with hanging folders or envelopes to hold photos. Consider the Digital Images folder to be the file cabinet, and the individual folders inside to be the equivalent of the file cabinet's hanging folders.

I select all the images in the memory card folder and drag them to this new folder. This copies all the images onto the hard drive and into my "filing cabinet," which is actually better than using a physical filing cabinet because, for example, I can use browser software to rename all the photos in that new folder, giving information about each photo (such as HorsetailFallsColGrgOR 01).

I also set up a group of folders in a separate "filing cabinet" (a new folder at the level of Digital Images) for edited photos. In this second filing cabinet, I include sub folders specific to types of photography, such as landscapes, close-ups, people, etc. Inside them, I can break down categories even further when that helps to organize my photos. Inside these sub categories I place copies of original images that I have examined and decided are definite keepers, both unprocessed (direct from the camera) and processed images (keeping such files separate). Make sure these are copies (rather than simply moving the files here), it is important to keep all "original" photo files in the original folder that they went to when first downloaded.

Once you have downloaded your images onto the computer, it helps to burn them to a quality CD as soon as possible. CDs take the place of negatives in the digital world. Storing your images only on your hard drive can make you vulnerable; you don't want your copies of an important photo project to be stored exclusively on your computer (something could happen to them). Set up a CD binder for your digital "negatives." You may want to keep your original and edited images on separate discs (or separate folders on the same disk). DVD is another alternative, although at this point, it is not 100% readable if you need to go from computer to computer.

Browser Programs

While the latest Photoshop has an improved browser that can help organize photos, it still doesn't do as well as software specifically made for this purpose. There are currently a number of programs that help view and organize your images.

ACDSee is a superb program with a customizable interface, keyboard tagging of images, and some unique characteristics such as a calendar feature that lets you find photos by date (though the best featured version is Windows only). Another very good program with similar capabilities is iView Media (with equal features on both Windows and Mac versions). You may also want to check out Digital PhotoPro, which was designed by professional photographers and has some interesting pro features, including a magnifying digital "loupe."

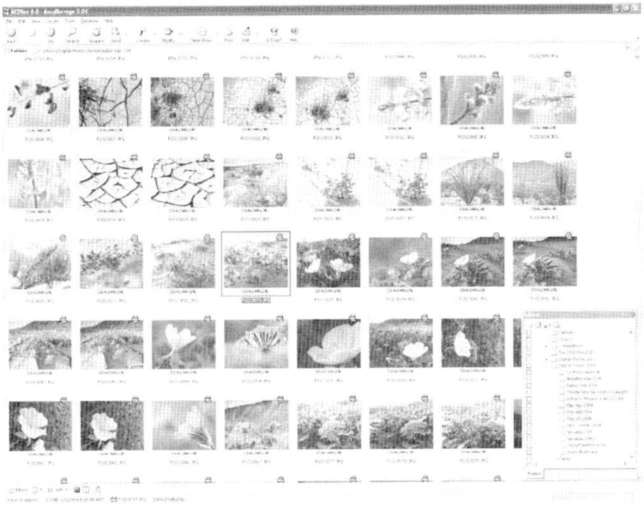

A browser not only allows you to see the images you have shot, but helps you manage them as well. Some of the functions offered by different programs include searching, moving and deleting files, listing information about the photo, and the ability to create index prints of file folders.

All of these browser programs include some database functions (such as keyword searches) and many will operate on both Windows and Mac platforms. These programs allow you to quickly look at photos on your computer, edit them, rename photos one at a time or all at once, read all major files, move photos from folder to folder, resize photos for e-mailing, create simple slideshows, and more.

An important function of browser programs is their ability to print customized index prints. You can then give a title to each of these index prints, and also list additional information about the photographer as well as the photo's file location. The index print is a hardcopy that allows easy reference (and visual searches). You could include an index print with every CD you burn so you can quickly see what is on the CD and find the file you need. A combination of uniquely labeled file folders on your hard drive, a browser program, and index prints will help you to maintain a fast and easy way of finding and sorting images.

Image Processing

Of course, you can process the 20D's JPEG files in any image-processing program. One nice thing about JPEG is that it is one of the most universally available formats. Any program on any computer that recognizes image files will recognize JPEG. That said, it is important to understand that the original JPEG file is more like a negative than a slide. Sure, you can use it directly, just like you could have the local mini-lab make prints from negatives. But JPEG files can be processed to get more out of them.

While RAW files offer more capacity for change, you can still do a lot with a JPEG file to optimize it for use. I shoot mainly JPEG for my professional work because it fits my workflow and personality, and no clients complain about the quality of my images.

RAW, as discussed earlier, is an important format because it increases the options for adjustment of your images. In addition, Canon's new RAW file, CR2, offers increased flexibility and control over the image. When shooting RAW, you have to work on every image, which does change your workflow. This is why photographers who sometimes, but not always, need to work with RAW will use the 20D's ability to record RAW and JPEG at the same time.

The big advantage to the RAW file is that it captures more directly what the sensor sees. It holds more information (12-bits vs. the standard 8-bits per color) and can have stronger correction applied to it (compared to JPEG images) without problems showing. This can be particularly helpful when there are difficulties with exposure or color balance. (Remember that the image file from the camera holds 12-bits of data even though it is contained in a 16-bit file—so while you can get a 16-bit TIFF file from the RAW file, it is based on 12 bits of data.)

Note: 20D RAW files are nearly 9 MB in size, so they will fill memory cards quite quickly. In addition, they can increase processing and workflow times.

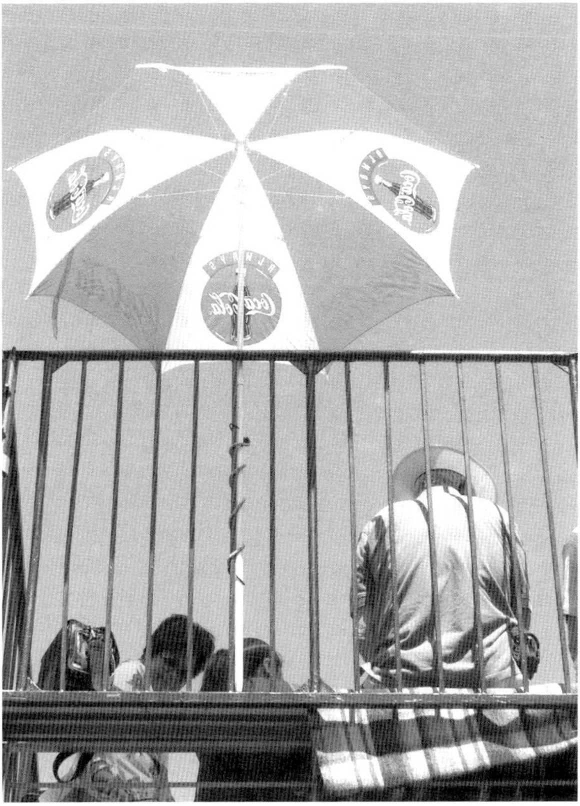

When shooting RAW files, you record more digital information than with other formats, which creates more options but requires more image processing after the shoot.

Canon offers two ways of converting CR2 files to standard files that can be optimized in Photoshop: the File Viewer Utility and the Digital Photo Professional software. In addition, Photoshop CS has a RAW converter built-in, and C1 software (from Phase One) has some high-level features for RAW conversion and workflow that many photographers like. There is a slight quality difference between using these and using the Canon software, which after all was created specifically for Canon's proprietary RAW file. However, the difference is small.

The File Viewer Utility

This software from Canon is easy to use. It is a good "browser" program that lets you view and organize RAW and JPEG files. It will convert RAW files, though it is a pretty simple program and doesn't offer some of the features available in other RAW processing software. Even so, it does a very good job of translating details from the RAW file into TIFF or JPEG form. Once converted, the new TIFF or JPEG files are readable by any image-processing program. TIFF is the preferred file format (JPEG would only be used if you had file space limitations). The File Viewer Utility supplied with the 20D is much faster than earlier versions. In addition, it includes EOS Capture, a remote capturing control that lets you work your camera remotely when attached to the computer.

Digital Photo Professional Software

Digital Photo Professional (DPP) was developed to bring Canon RAW file processing up to speed with the rest of the digital world (even Canon admitted the File Viewer Utility did not have the power of competitive programs, yet it was their only RAW conversion program). This optional program has a brand-new processing engine and will work on all EOS-1D series cameras as well as the 20D plus the Digital Rebel. It can be used to process both CR2 files and JPEG files. The advantage to processing JPEG files is that DPP is quicker and easier to use than Photoshop, yet is still quite powerful. So for fast and simple JPEG processing, DPP works quite well. I believe if you are going to shoot RAW, this is a must-use program. It is fast, full-featured and gives excellent results.

Storing Your Images

Even though digital images are stored as digital files, they can still be lost or destroyed without proper care. Many photographers use two hard drives, either adding a second one to the inside of the computer or using an external USB or FireWire drive. This allows you to immediately and easily back-up photos on the second drive. It is very rare for two drives to fail at once (though it is still highly recommended that you burn your images to CD).

Hard drives and memory cards are all devices known as magnetic media. As such, they do a great job at recording image files for processing, transmitting, sharing, and more. However, they are not good for long-term storage. Magnetic media have a limited life. Most manufacturers won't rate such storage devices beyond 10 years. This is a conservative number, to be sure, but this type of media has been known to lose data in that time span.

There are also a number of malicious computer viruses that can wipe out image files from a hard drive (especially JPEGs). Even the best drives can crash, rendering them unusable. Plus, we are all capable of accidentally erasing or saving over an important photo.

The answer to these storage problems today is optical media. A CD-writer (or "burner") is a necessity for the digital photographer. DVD-writers work extremely well, too, and DVDs can handle about six times the data that can be saved on a CD. Either option allows you to back up photo files and store images safely.

There are two types of disk media that can be used for recording data: R designated (i.e. CD-R or DVD-R) recordable disks; and RW designated (i.e. CD-RW or DVD-RW) rewritable disks. CD-R disks can only be recorded once—they cannot be erased and no new images can be added to them. CD-RWs, on the other hand, can be recorded on and then erased and reused later, and you can add more data to them as well.

However, if you want long-term storage of your images, use CD-R disks rather than CD-RWs (the latter is best used for temporary storage, as when transporting images to a new location). The storage medium used for CD-R disks is more stable than that of CD-RWs (which makes sense since the CD-RWs are designed to be erasable).

Buy quality media. Inexpensive disks may not preserve your photo-image files as long as you would like them to. Read the box. Look for information about the life of the disk. Most long-lived disks are labeled as such and cost a little more.

Direct Printing

With certain compatible Canon printers, you can control the printing directly from the 20D. Simply connect the camera to the printer using the dedicated USB cord that came with the printer. Canon printers that allow direct printing include the standard Bubble Jet printers (Bubble Jet is Canon's ink jet technology).

In addition, the camera is PictBridge compatible (meaning that it can be directly connected to PictBridge printers from several manufacturers). Nearly all new photo printers are PictBridge compatible. With these printers, you use the USB cord that came with the camera.

Note: RAW files cannot be used for the direct printing options mentioned in this section.

To start the process, first set the camera to communicate with the printer. Do this in the Set-up menu under *Communications*—then select *PTP*. Next, making sure that both the camera and the printer are turned off, connect the camera to the printer with the camera's USB cord (the connections are straightforward since the plugs only work one way). Turn on the printer first, then the camera—this lets the camera recognize the printer so it is prepared to control it (some printers may turn on automatically when the power cable is connected). Depending on the printer, the actual direct printing features of the camera will vary.

Press the Playback button ▶ and use the Quick Control Dial to select an image on the LCD Monitor that you want to print. There will be an icon in the upper left to indicate the printer is connected. Press the SET button and the Print Setting screen will appear, giving such printing choices as whether to imprint the date, to include effects, number of copies, trimming area, and paper settings (size, type, borders or borderless). Continue to use the Quick Control Dial and SET button to set these options to the desired settings. These choices may change depending on the printer; refer to the printer's manual if necessary.

Trimming is a neat choice because it allows you to actually crop your photo right in the LCD Monitor before printing, so you can tighten up the composition if needed.

Note: The amount of control you have over the image when printing directly from the camera is limited entirely by the printer, and often you will have little or no control over color and brightness. If you really need image control, print from the computer.

If you are shooting a lot of images for which you plan to use direct printing, do some test shots and set up the 20D's processing parameters to optimize the prints before actually shooting the final pictures. You may even want to create a custom setting that increases sharpness and saturation just for this purpose.

Digital Print Order Format (DPOF)

Another printing feature of the 20D is DPOF (Digital Print Order Format). This allows you to decide which images to print before you actually do any printing. Then, if you have a printer that recognizes DPOF, it will print those specifically chosen images automatically. It is also a way to select images on a memory card for printing at a photo lab. When you drop off your CF card with images selected using DPOF—assuming the lab's equipment recognizes DPOF (ask before you leave your card)—the lab will know which prints you want.

DPOF is accessible through the Playback menu under *Print Order*. You can set the options you want, choosing all or any combination of individual images. Select *Set Up* to choose *Print Type* (standard or index), *Date* (on or off), and *File No.* (on or off). After setting up your choices, press the MENU tab on the display to return to *Print Order*. From there, select to choose either *Order* or *All* and release. *Order* allows you to use the Quick Control Dial to select which individual images you want to print, along with their quantity (*All* selects all the images on the card for printing). RAW files cannot be selected for DPOF printing.

Glossary

aberration
An optical flaw in a lens that causes the image to be distorted or unclear.

Adobe Photoshop
Professional-level image-processing software with extremely powerful filter and color-correction tools. It offers features for photography, graphic design, web design, and video.

Adobe Photoshop Elements
A photo-processing program based on the processing "engine" of Photoshop (though it has a different interface and set of controls). The Elements program lacks some of the more sophisticated controls available in Photoshop, but it does have a comprehensive range of image-manipulation options.

AE
See automatic exposure.

AF
See automatic focus.

AI
Automatic Indexing.

ambient light
See available light.

angle of view
The area seen by a lens, usually measured in degrees across the diagonal of the film frame.

anti-aliasing
A technique that reduces or eliminates the jagged appearance of lines or edges in an image.

aperture
The opening in the lens that allows light to enter the camera. Aperture is usually described as an f/number. The higher the f/number, the smaller the aperture; and the lower the f/number, the larger the aperture.

Aperture-Priority mode
A type of automatic exposure in which you manually select the aperture and the camera automatically selects the shutter speed.

artifact
Information that is not part of the scene but appears in the image due to technology. Artifacts can occur in film or digital images and include grain, flare, static marks, color flaws, noise, etc.

artificial light
Usually refers to any light source that doesn't exist in nature, such as incandescent, fluorescent, and other manufactured lighting.

automatic exposure
When the camera measures light and makes the adjustments necessary to create proper image density on sensitized media.

automatic flash
An electronic flash unit that reads light reflected off a subject (from either a preflash or the actual flash exposure), then shuts itself off as soon as ample light has reached the sensitized medium.

automatic focus
When the camera automatically adjusts the lens elements to sharply render the subject.

Av
Aperture Value. See Aperture-priority mode.

available light
The amount of illumination at a given location that applies to natural and artificial light sources but not those supplied specifically for photography. It is also called existing light or ambient light.

backlight
Light that projects toward the camera from behind the subject.

backup
A copy of a file or program made to ensure that, if the original is lost or damaged, the necessary information is still intact.

barrel distortion
A defect in the lens that makes straight lines curve outward away from the middle of the image — most noticeable toward the edges of the frame.

bit
Binary digit. This is the basic unit of binary computation. See also, byte.

bit depth
The number of bits per pixel that determines the number of colors the image can display. Eight bits per pixel is the minimum requirement for a photo-quality color image.

bounce light
Light that reflects off of another surface before illuminating the subject.

bracketing
A sequence of pictures taken of the same subject but varying one or more exposure settings, manually or automatically, between each exposure.

brightness
A subjective measure of illumination. See also, luminance.

buffer
Temporarily stores data so that other programs, on the camera or the computer, can continue to run while data is in transition.

built-in flash
A flash that is permanently attached to the camera body. The built-in flash will pop up and fire in low-light situations when using the camera's automated exposure settings.

built-in meter
A light-measuring device that is incorporated into the camera body.

bulb
A camera setting that allows the shutter to stay open as long as the shutter release is depressed.

byte
A single group of eight bits that is processed as one unit. See also, bit.

card reader
Device that connects to your computer and enables quick and easy download of images from memory card to computer.

CCD
Charge Coupled Device. This is a common digital camera sensor type that is sensitized by applying an electrical charge to the sensor prior to its exposure to light. It converts light energy into an electrical impulse.

chromatic aberration
Occurs when light rays of different colors are focused on different planes, causing colored halos around objects in the image.

chrominance
A component of an image that expresses the color (hue and saturation) information, as opposed to the luminance (lightness) values.

close-up
A general term used to describe an image created by closely focusing on a subject. Often involves the use of special lenses or extension tubes.

CMOS
Complementary Metal Oxide Semiconductor. Like CCD sensors, this sensor type converts light into an electrical impulse. CMOS sensors are similar to CCDs, are less expensive to produce, and use less power. See also, CCD.

CMYK mode
Cyan, magenta, yellow, and black. This mode is typically used in image-editing applications when preparing an image for printing.

color balance
The average overall color in a reproduced image. How a digital camera interprets the color of light in a scene so that white or neutral gray appear neutral.

color cast
A colored hue over the image often caused by improper lighting or incorrect white balance settings. Can be produced intentionally for creative effect.

color space
A mapped relationship between colors and computer data about the colors.

CompactFlash (CF) card
One of the most widely used removable memory cards.

complementary colors
In theory: any two colors of light that, when combined, emit all known light wavelengths, resulting in white light. Also, it can be any pair of dye or pigment colors that absorb all known light wavelengths, resulting in black.

compression
A method of reducing file size through removal of redundant data, as with the JPEG file format.

contrast
The difference between two or more tones in terms of luminance, density, or darkness.

contrast filter
A colored filter that lightens or darkens the monotone representation of a colored area or object in a black-and-white photograph.

critical focus
The most sharply focused plane within an image.

cropping
The process of extracting a portion of the image area. If this portion of the image is enlarged, pixels are spread out, effectively lowering resolution.

dedicated flash
An electronic flash unit that talks with the camera, communicating things such as flash illumination, lens focal length, subject distance, and sometimes flash status.

default
Refers to various factory-set attributes or features, which in the case of a camera, includes controls that can be changed by the user but can, as desired, be reset to the original factory settings.

depth of field
The image space in front of and behind the plane of focus that appears acceptably sharp in the photograph — the sharpness in depth from front to back in an image.

diaphragm
A mechanism that determines the size of the lens opening that allows light to pass into the camera when taking a photo.

diopter
A measurement of the refractive power of a lens element — this is typically used to identify the amount of correction at the eyepiece to allow the photographer to better see the viewfinder. Also, it may be a supplementary lens that is defined by its focal length and power of magnification.

download
The transfer of data from one device to another, such as from camera to computer or computer to printer.

dpi
Dots per inch. Used to define the resolution of a printer, this term refers to the number of dots of ink that a printer can lay down in an inch. It is commonly used interchangeably with PPI, because it also refers to the pixels in a scanner, meaning it is then directly related to the pixels in an image.

DPOF
Digital Print Order Format. A feature that enables the camera to supply data about the printing of image files and supplementary information contained within them. The printer must be DPOF compatible for the system to operate.

dye sublimation printer
Creates color on the printed page by vaporizing inks that then solidify on the page.

electronic flash
A device with a glass or plastic tube filled with gas that, when electrified, creates an intense flash of light.

electronic rangefinder
A system that utilizes the AF technology built into a camera to provide a visual confirmation that focus has been achieved. It can operate in either manual or AF focus modes.

EV
Exposure value. A number that quantifies the amount of light within a scene, allowing you to determine the relative combinations of aperture and shutter speed to accurately reproduce the light levels of that exposure.

EXIF
Exchangeable Image File Format. This format is used for storing an image file's interchange information.

exposure
When light enters a camera and reacts with the sensitized medium. It also refers to the amount of light that strikes the sensitized medium.

exposure meter
See light meter.

extension tube
A hollow metal ring that can be fitted between the camera and lens (it usually includes mechanical and electronic connectors so the camera and lens still work normally). It increases the distance between the optical center of the lens and the sensor and decreases the minimum focus distance of the lens.

FAT
File Allocation Table. This is a method used by computer operating systems to keep track of files stored on the hard drive.

file format
The form in which digital images are stored and recorded, e.g., JPEG, RAW, TIFF, etc.

filter
A piece of plastic or glass used to control how certain wavelengths of light are recorded. A filter absorbs selected wavelengths, preventing them from reaching the sensitized medium. Also, software available in image-processing computer programs that produce special filter effects.

FireWire
A high speed data transfer standard that allows outlying accessories to be plugged and unplugged from the computer while it is turned on. Some digital cameras and card readers use FireWire to connect to the computer. FireWire transfers data faster than USB. See also, Mbps.

firmware
Software that is permanently incorporated into a hardware chip. All computer-based equipment, including digital cameras, use firmware of some kind.

flare
Unwanted light streaks or rings that appear in the viewfinder, on the recorded image, or both. It is caused by extraneous light entering the lens and camera during shooting. Diffuse flare is uniformly reflected light that can lower the contrast of the image. Zoom lenses are especially susceptible to flare because they are comprised of many elements. Filters can also increase flare. Use of a lens hood can often reduce this undesirable effect.

f/number
See f/stop.

focal length
When the lens is focused on infinity, it is the distance from the optical center of the lens to the focal plane.

focal plane
The plane on which a lens forms a sharp image. Also, it may be the film plane or sensor plane.

focus
An optimum sharpness or image clarity that occurs when a lens creates a sharp image by converging light rays to specific points at the focal plane. The word also refers to the act of adjusting the lens to achieve optimal image sharpness.

FP high-speed sync
Focal Plane high-speed sync. This allows flash units to be synchronized at shutter speeds higher than the standard sync speed. In this flash mode, the level of flash output is reduced and, consequently, the shooting range is reduced.

f/stop
The size of the aperture or diaphragm opening of a lens, also referred to as f/number or stop. The term stands for the ratio of the focal length (f) of the lens to the width of its aperture opening – while this ratio actually is a fraction, the f-stop number does not use a fraction, but simply the denominator, which is why f/2.8 is a wide opening

(1/2.8) compared to f22 being a narrow opening (1/22). Each stop up (lower f/number) doubles the amount of light reaching the sensitized medium. Each stop down (higher f/number) halves the amount of light reaching the sensitized medium.

full-frame
The maximum area of the sensitized medium (film or sensor) that can be used by the camera.

full-sized sensor
A sensor in a digital camera that has the same dimensions as a 35mm film frame (24 x 36 mm).

GB
See gigabyte.

gigabyte
Just over one billion bytes.

GN
See guide number.

gray card
A card used to take accurate exposure readings. It typically has a gray side that reflects 18% (which is visually middle gray) and a white side that reflects 90% of the light.

gray scale
A successive series of tones ranging between black and white, which have no color.

guide number
A number used to quantify the output of a flash unit. It is derived by using this formula: GN = aperture x distance. Guide numbers are expressed for a given ISO film speed in either feet or meters.

hard drive
A contained storage unit made up of magnetically sensitive disks.

histogram
A graphic representation of image tones.

hot shoe
An electronically connected flash mount on the camera body. It enables direct connection between the camera and an external flash, and synchronizes the shutter release with the firing of the flash.

icon
A symbol used to represent a file, function, or program.

image-editing program
See image-processing program

image-processing program
Software that allows for image adjustment, alteration and enhancement.

infinity
In photographic terms, the theoretical most distant point of focus.

interpolation
Process used to increase image resolution by creating new pixels based on existing pixels. The software intelligently looks at existing pixels and creates new pixels to fill the gaps and achieve a higher resolution.

IS
Image Stabilization. This is a technology that reduces camera shake and vibration. It is used in lenses, binoculars, camcorders, etc. Canon uses this name; Nikon's is Vibration Reduction; Minolta uses Anti-Shake, and Sigma has chosen Optical Stabilization.

ISO
A term for industry standards from the International Organization for Standardization. When an ISO number is applied to film, it indicates the relative light sensitivity of the recording medium. Digital sensors use film ISO equivalents, which are based on enhancing the data stream or boosting the signal.

JPEG
Joint Photographic Experts Group. This is a lossy compression file format that works with any computer and photo software. JPEG smartly examines an image for redundant information, removes it for storage, then rebuilds the data later when the file is opened in the computer. It is a variable compression format because the amount of data in the file depends on the detail in the photo and the amount of compression. At low compression/high quality, the loss of data has a negligible effect on the photo. However, JPEG should not be used as a working format—the file should be reopened and saved in a format such as TIFF, which does not compress the image.

KB
See kilobyte.

kilobyte
Just over one thousand bytes.

LCD
Liquid Crystal Display; a flat screen with two polarizing sheets on either side of a liquid crystal solution. When activated by an electric current, the LCD uses the crystals to either pass through or block light, creating a colored image.

LED
Light Emitting Diode. It is a light often employed as an indicator on cameras as well as on other electronic equipment.

lens
The optics in front of a camera that have been designed for photo use with multiple glass elements to control angle of view (focal length) and sharp images on the sensor or film.

lens hood
Also called a lens shade. This is a short tube that can be attached to the front of a lens to reduce flare. It keeps undesirable light from reaching the front of the lens and also protects the front of the lens.

lens shade
See lens hood.

light meter
Also called an exposure meter, it is a device that measures light levels and calculates the correct aperture and shutter speed.

lithium-ion
A popular battery technology (sometimes abbreviated to Li-ion) that is not prone to the charge memory effects of nickel-cadmium (Ni-Cd) batteries or the low temperature performance problems of alkaline batteries.

long lens
See telephoto lens.

lossless
Image compression in which no data is lost.

lossy
Image compression in which data is lost and, thereby, image quality may be lessened. This means that the greater the compression, the lesser the image quality.

luminance
A term used to describe directional brightness. See also, brightness, chrominance, and noise.

luminance noise
A form of noise that appears as a sprinkling of black "grain" in an image.

M
See Manual Exposure mode.

macro lens
A lens designed to be at top sharpness over a flat field when focused at close distances and reproduction ratios up to 1:1.

main light
The primary or dominant light source. It influences texture, volume, and shadows.

Manual Exposure mode
A camera operating mode that requires the user to determine and set both the aperture and shutter speed. This is the opposite of automatic exposure.

MB
See megabyte.

Mbps
Megabits per second. This unit is used to describe the rate of data transfer. See also, megabit.

megabit
One million bits of data. See also, bit.

megabyte
Just over one million bytes.

megapixel
A million pixels.

memory
The storage capacity of a hard drive or other recording media.

memory card
A solid state removable storage medium used in digital devices. They can store still images, moving images, or sound, as well as related file data. There are several different types, including CompactFlash, xD, or Sony's proprietary Memory Stick, to name a few. Individual card capacity is limited by available storage as well as by the

size of the recorded data (determined by factors such as image resolution and file format). See also, CompactFlash (CF) card, file format.

menu
A listing of features, functions, or options displayed on a screen that can be selected and activated by the user.

middle gray
Halfway between black and white, it is an average gray tone with 18% reflectance. See also, gray card.

midtone
The tone that appears as medium brightness, or medium gray tone, in a photographic print.

mode
Specified operating conditions of the camera or software program.

moiré
A moiré pattern occurs because the "frequency" of detail in a scene conflicts with the resolution on a sensor. Moiré appears as a wavy pattern over the image.

noise
The digital equivalent of grain. It is often caused by a number of different factors, such as a high ISO setting, heat, sensor design, etc. Though usually undesirable, it may be added for creative effect using an image-processing program. See also, chrominance noise and luminance noise.

normal lens
See standard lens.

operating system (OS)
The system software that provides the environment within which all other software operates.

overexposed
When too much light is recorded with the image, causing the photo to be too light or washed out in tone.

pan
Moving the camera to follow a moving subject. When a slow shutter speed is used, this creates an image in which the subject appears sharp and the background is blurred.

perspective
The effect of the distance between the camera and image elements upon the perceived size of objects in an image. It is also an expression of this three-dimensional relationship in two dimensions.

pixel
Derived from picture element. A pixel is the base component of a digital image. Every individual pixel can have a distinct color and tone.

plug-in
Third-party software created to augment an existing software program.

polarization
An effect achieved by using a polarizing filter. It minimizes reflections from non-metallic surfaces like water and glass and saturates colors by removing glare. Polarization often makes skies appear bluer at 90 degrees to the sun. The term also applies to the above effects simulated by a polarizing software filter.

pre-flash
Short duration, low intensity flash pulse emitted by a flash unit immediately prior to the shutter opening. This allows the TTL light meter to assess the reflectivity of the subject and determine flash exposure.
See also, TTL.

Program mode
In Program exposure mode, the camera selects a combination of shutter speed and aperture automatically.

RAM
Stands for Random Access Memory, which is a computer's memory capacity, directly accessible from the central processing unit.

RAW
An image file format that has little or no internal processing applied by the camera. It contains 12-bit color information, a wider range of data than 8-bit formats such as JPEG.

RAW+JPEG
An image file format not a format – it is a file recording choice that records two files per capture; one RAW file and one JPEG file.

rear curtain sync
A feature that causes the flash unit to fire just prior to the shutter closing. It is used for creative effect when mixing flash and ambient light.

resolution
The amount of data available for an image as applied to image size. It is expressed in pixels or megapixels, or sometimes as lines per inch on a monitor or dots per inch on a printed image.

RGB mode
Red, Green, and Blue. This is the color model most commonly used to display color images on video systems, film recorders, and computer monitors. It displays all visible colors as combinations of red, green, and blue. RGB mode is the most common color mode for viewing and working with digital files onscreen.

saturation
The degree to which a color of fixed tone varies from the neutral, grey tone; low saturation produces pastel shades whereas high saturation gives pure color.

sharp
A term used to describe the quality of an image as clear,

crisp, and perfectly focused, as opposed to fuzzy, obscure, or unfocused.

short lens
A lens with a short focal length—a wide-angle lens. It produces a greater angle of view than a normal lens.

shutter
The apparatus that controls the amount of time during which light is allowed to reach the film or sensor.

Shutter-Priority mode
An automatic exposure mode in which you manually select the shutter speed and the camera automatically selects the aperture.

Single-lens reflex
See SLR.

slow sync
A flash mode in which a slow shutter speed is used with the flash in order to allow low-level ambient light to be recorded by the film or sensor.

SLR
Single-lens reflex. A camera with mirror that reflects the image from the lens onto the viewfinder screen. A pentaprism or pentamirror then allows you to see that screen through the eyepiece. When you take the picture, the mirror reflexes out of the way, the focal plane shutter opens, and the image is recorded.

small-format sensor
In some digital cameras, this type of sensor is physically smaller than the 35mm film frame. The result is that lenses cover a smaller angle of view than on a 34mm camera. In effect, they act like longer lenses. This is because the sensor covers a smaller area or angle of view than would be seen by the full-frame 35mm and the same lens. Note — the sensor cannot see an angle of view smaller than that of the lens.

standard lens
Also known as a normal lens, this is a fixed-focal-length lens usually in the range of 45 to 55mm for 35mm format (or the equivalent range for small-format sensors). In contrast to wide-angle or telephoto lenses, a standard lens views a realistically proportionate perspective of a scene.

stop down
To reduce the size of the diaphragm opening by using a higher f/number.

stop up
To increase the size of the diaphragm opening by using a lower f/number.

strobe
Abbreviation for stroboscopic. An electronic light source that produces a series of evenly spaced bursts of light. Often used to refer to any electronic flash.

synchronize
Causing a flash unit to fire simultaneously with the complete opening of the camera's shutter.

telephoto effect
When objects in an image appear closer than they really are through the use of a telephoto lens.

telephoto lens
A lens with a long focal length that enlarges the subject and produces a narrower angle of view than you would see with your eyes.

thumbnail
A small representation of an image file used principally for identification purposes.

TIFF
Tagged Image File Format. This popular digital format uses no compression, is a ubiquitous format that both Mac and Windows platforms recognize, and will not affect the image when opened and resaved repeatedly.

tripod
A three-legged stand that stabilizes the camera and eliminates camera shake caused by body movement or vibration. Tripods are usually adjustable for height and angle.

TTL
Through-the-Lens, i.e. TTL metering.

Tv
Time Value.
See Shutter-Priority mode.

USB
Universal Serial Bus. This interface standard allows outlying accessories to be plugged and unplugged from the computer while it is turned on. USB 2.0 enables high-speed data transfer.

vignetting
A reduction in light at the edge of an image due to use of a filter or an inappropriate lens hood. This can also occur by using a small-format lens on a larger-format digital camera.

viewfinder screen
The ground glass surface on which you view your image.

wide-angle lens
A lens that lets you see a scene with an angle of view wider than the typical standard or normal lens. See also, short lens.

Wi-Fi
Wireless Fidelity, a technology that allows for wireless networking between one Wi-Fi compatible product and another.

zoom lens
A lens that adjusts to cover a wide range of focal lengths.

Index